THE IMPERFECT VIEW

by

Russell F. Conran

Chrysler Books
Box 243
Marne, MI 49435

THE IMPERFECT VIEW

ISBN 0-9633908-4-8

Credits:

Cover picture by

Russell F. Conran

Editor

Illana Olsen

Chrysler Books
Box 243
Marne, MI 49435

- Dedication -

Happily and gratefully, in acknowledgment of her patience, her understanding, her supportive attitude, and her willingness to do my typewriting, I dedicate this book to my wife of 50 years, Vivienne (McConeghy) Conran.

Introduction

Over the years I have spent a lot of time with my grandparents. One of my favorite parts of my visits with them is to sit at my grandfather's feet and listen to him tell stories of his childhood or read aloud the stories and poems he has written. I loved listening to him as a child, and I still do now.

As I grew up, it became increasingly apparent to me that Grandfather is a singular individual. He has a unique ability to make people laugh. However, he is equally good at making them think seriously, and even cry. Some of his stories caused me to do all three.

It doesn't surprise me that he has always been popular as a public speaker. His well of humor and insight has never run dry. He has commented on politics, science, world events, social happenings and numerous other topics for over forty years, all with his special brand of wit and wisdom, frequently flavored with a bit of pepper.

These are stories you'll want to read and re-read, and laugh over. After all, that was why they were written -- to make people laugh.

It has long been a dream of mine to see my grandfather's work in print. It gives me a deep sense of satisfaction that it has finally come to pass.

Enjoy!
Illana A. Olsen

Table of Contents

I   STORIES

Table of Contents

Preface

First off, to deal fairly with the reading public, there are no references to sex in this book. That being acknowledged, if you can accept your disappointment in good grace, and will still purchase a copy, you will find in its pages humor of a character that could induce you to smile in amusement, chuckle in delight, or even break into laughter. While no substitute for sex, humor might rate a distant second among life's many pleasures.

Over many years, for divers reasons and purposes, I've written stories, poems, skits and more to record my personal thoughts and ideas, to amuse audiences, for the purpose of public speaking, and in response to requests, a good part of which is recorded in this book.

With some frequency I've been asked, "Why don't you publish your writings?" That desire grew in me as time passed, and here late in life, with the assistance of my granddaughter Illana Olsen, that desire has become reality.

May the reader find pleasure in its perusal.

Russell F. Conran

About is my yardstick whenever I make or repair things. If six inches is the requirement, about six inches will do fine. I've never had the time in my "un-busy" life to strive for precision. Of course, if instead of about, I happen to cut out the exact length or width or thickness required, I decide on the spot that I have licked my problem, and vow to be precise thereafter--which I am never able to be.

Being the "abouter" that I am, I am, of course, somewhat of an expert in compensating for pieces too short; and forcing into place pieces too long, too wide or too thick, which I view as a skill worthy of my incapability.

I am consoled in the belief that I am not alone with my unskillful techniques. I have an urge to found a lodge with membership open only to "abouters" meeting say, about once a month, with dues say about $10.00, with a membership of say about 50, to foster and promote abouting with programs about about, abouters, and abouting. Wanna join?

STORIES

LOVE OUTSIDE HOLLYWOOD   1982

The Hatton family was childless, and consisted of husband Hazen and wife Delia. Hazen and Delia were presently twenty years into marriage despite predictions to the contrary. Both were plain persons of no great charm or talent. Both had been overlooked in the pairings that resulted in marriage until they found themselves left much like the unwanted apples in the bushel. If this seems an odd way to bring together a couple made for each other, after twenty years it would appear to have been a good one. After all, true love has no scruples about choosing in whose hearts it will reside. Hasn't it often spurned residence in the hearts of the rich, the mighty and the ambitious?

It was Sunday afternoon, and Hazen was lounging in his favorite chair immersed in a football game on television, while digesting a savory meal prepared and served by Delia. He was in that comfortable state of mind and body where he might have fallen asleep had not there been a succession of undecipherable and unusual sounds coming from the kitchen where Delia was supposedly completing her after-dinner chores. Kept awake and wondering what on earth was going on out there, Hazen, fighting back the feeling that he should find out, and doing it successfully up to the present moment, was startled out of his lethargy when came Delia's shrill voice from that direction.

"Hazen! The kitchen drain is plugged up. Will you get out here and see what you can do about it? and right now!", she added with emphasis, as if supplying more propellant to a rocket for faster launching.

Hazen had been summoned like this hundreds of times in those twenty years of marriage, and no longer bounded up in response as he once did. Besides, the football game was at a decisive point, and he was loath to leave it; so he pretended not to have heard and remained stationary.

"HAZEN!! YOU EITHER GET OUT HERE NOW, OR YOU CAN EAT OFF DIRTY DISHES UNTIL YOU DO! DO YOU HEAR ME?"

Ignoring this last summons was more than Hazen had courage to do, so he ambled kitchenward, stuck his head in the doorway, and pretending to be uncertain about being wanted, with feigned innocence asked: "Did you call me, dear?"

"Did I call him, he wants to know! Did I call him!" she repeated with sarcasm. "Are you wearing your ears? I ask. Of course I called you! Get out here and see what you can do about unplugging this miserable drain. I can't free it, and I've tried everything I can think of. The plunger won't loosen it either. Maybe you can fix it," she said in a tone that indicated serious doubt.

"Maybe you can fix it." That qualified expression of confidence in a husband's ability, even when stated in an uncivil tone of voice, as this was, can be a tonic to the male ego. No exhortation could do more in getting action. Hazen heard, and was immediately ready and willing to supply his expertise--if what he had to offer could in any way be so labeled. He walked over to the sink, gave it his keen scrutiny, ran a little water to confirm Delia's contention that the drain was plugged, satisfied himself on that point, turned around to Delia and asked: "Just what have you been stuffin' down it anyway?"

If females have egos, they are rarely acknowledged, but they do have sensitivity in generous supply. With temper rising and eyes blazing in resentment, Delia responded. "The same stuff you stuffed down your throat at dinner time, that's what I stuffed down it!"

"Humph!" said Hazen unaffected. "I got it down all right."

So powerful at that moment was Delia's urge to make an unflattering comparison between the drain pipe and Hazen's gullet that she restrained herself only with great difficulty. Holding back, she came out with: "Are you just gonna stand there and infer it's my fault because the drain is plugged, or are you gonna do something about it?"

Having, by implication, tossed blame Delia's way, his much-battered sense of superiority blown up accordingly, Hazen took command. "What you need here is some of that drain cleaner they keep showin' on TV. What's it called--I can't think."

"How would I know which one you mean?" asked Delia. "They show a half-dozen different ones."

"Oh, you know that one where the half-covered woman bends over the sink, and you forget all about what they're advertising, 'cause you wonder if she'll lose---"

"That's enough of that kind of talk!" said Delia interrupting. "Those ads don't sell me on a product."

"I know that," said Hazen. "I just brought it up hoping it would remind you of the name of that drain cleaner."

"Do you mean UnPlug-O?", asked Delia.

"Yeah, that's it. That's the stuff I meant."

"I haven't got any," said Delia.

"It's cleaned all the drains on TV," said Hazen, "it oughta clean this one."

"I doubt it!" said Delia tersely.

"That store on the corner is open on Sunday. Guess I'll run down there and get a can of it," said Hazen.

"If you want your supper on time, you'd better make it snappy," said Delia as Hazen went out the back door.

Hazen was not gone long. When he returned, Delia was in the bedroom making the bed and straightening up the room. Alone in the kitchen, he took it upon himself to go ahead. He opened the can, poured all its contents into the offending drain in careless disregard of explicit instructions on the label, ran some water over the chemical, and stood nearby to await the results, smugly confident it would perform up to expectations.

Gurgling noises came almost at once; hiccups followed, then came a series of coughing sounds followed by a powerful belch that sent refuse ceilingward with the force of a cannon shot. The drain was unplugged, that was sure.

Hazen stepped up to the sink to confirm that it was unplugged. He was so pleased with himself that he could scarcely refrain from shouting. If he appeared completely indifferent to side effects and gave no thought to portentous results, that was Hazen's way. He stood there beside the sink exulting inside as bits and pieces of Sunday's dinner dropped on him from above like a rain of pestilence upon a sinner. They fell on the counter, on the floor as well as on that head wherein poor judgment held a lifetime lease.

Delia came running. The noise had reached her ears. She stopped in the doorway appalled and speechless, hands on hips, surveying the awful scene, her anger rising like a tide.

"There you are, dear," said Hazen, pleased and proud and expecting praise with a confidence that defied reason. "It's cleaned out now." This he added as more refuse fell on him. "I did the job! I did it!" he added exultingly.

Meantime, Delia had covered her face with her hands to hide her anger and to obscure the sight of the mess. She was breathing hard in an effort to control her feelings, and barely succeeding.

"It's as clean as a whistle," said Hazen, still awaiting her commendation. "That UnPlug-0 is great stuff! Boy, did it ever work!" His face was glowing with a look of triumph and self-satisfaction as he bent his head forward to look under Delia's hand as if to determine her reaction. Delia, peering between fingers, saw all this as she fought to control her anger.

"I did it for you! I got the drain fixed as good as new," added Hazen, somewhat perplexed that Delia had said nothing. "It won't give you any more trouble now," he went on with the obvious intent of coaxing from Delia the thanks and appreciation he so badly sought.

During these last few seconds, Delia had a lid on her anger and uncovered her face. She looked at her husband carefully and suddenly saw in his place a little boy, entreating his mother for praise; needing a pat on the head, a kiss on the cheek and a "good boy" reward for dubious achievement. Now in full control of herself, she stepped to the towel rack, took the towel from it, walked over to Hazen, and began wiping the worst of the splotches from his homely face. With a tear in her wifely eye she kissed that cleaned cheek most tenderly and spoke with a voice overflowing with emotion!

"Thank you, Hazen," she said, "for cleaning the drain for me. You really did a good job. Now go and shower and change your clothes like a good boy." She then turned to watch him as he left the room, swaggering in elation. It was then she again faced the mess he had made and cried. In a few moments she stopped crying, plopped herself down in a chair and began laughing hysterically. When that mood subsided, she wiped her eyes on the towel she still held, and to vindicate her conflicting emotions, said out loud: "Love makes no sense anyway," and began the task before her, as Hazen's cracked voice came from the bathroom in happy song.

THE FIRST UNCLE OSCAR STORY   1954

Speaking of Uncle Oscar, perhaps you would be interested in hearing how he made his money. It's a typical American success story which could be entitled "THE LUCKY STIFF" or "WHY DID IT HAVE TO HAPPEN TO HIM?" I'll tell you about it.

Uncle Oscar was an average man, he always paid his alimony, always closed the cover on the book of matches before striking one, owed the bank, and always voted "yes" at meetings, But fate had him in mind for better things.

One dark night some years ago, Uncle Oscar was driving down a remote country road in his 1940 Chevrolet following a heavy truck which had a protruding length of steel pipe. As the two vehicles rounded a curve in the road they came suddenly on a brightly lighted farmhouse. As rarely happens, the farmer's sixteen year old daughter was undressing in the upstairs bedroom at that moment, without drawing the shade, thus creating a terrific traffic hazard. Now, this truck driver happened to be a cad and a bounder, a regular pervert, who slammed on his brakes to prolong the sight just as Uncle Oscar, who was as bashful as a ten year old boy, shut his eyes to the view. In the confusion which followed these things took place in this order: The truck with the dangling pipe stopped abruptly, Uncle Oscar struck the pipe dangling from the truck with his 1940 Chevrolet, ramming the pipe through the radiator into the motor where it snapped off, the farmer's daughter drew her shade, and the farmer came running out of his house to see what was responsible for all the clatter. At this point the truck driver, seeing the damage he had caused by his perverted interest, and sensing correctly that Uncle Oscar's car was beyond running, sped away into the darkness like a thief in the night, leaving Uncle Oscar in a dazed condition with a piece of pipe through the radiator of his car and penetrating the motor.

As if this weren't enough to happen to a man in one night, the farmer at this juncture had the temerity to extend to Uncle Oscar an invitation to stay the night in his home. Luckily for Uncle Oscar he had heard about the farmer's daughter from a traveling salesman and didn't fall into the trap. As his head cleared, Uncle Oscar began to work frantically on his badly damaged car, and it is not surprising that after a time the faithful old vehicle responded to his efforts and started. Quickly, with relief, Uncle Oscar slipped behind the wheel and drove off into the night toward the city.

You can imagine what a spectacle he made. Here he was in this damaged car which made noises that would in no way be associated with automobiles, a sort of diabolical coughing and wheezing interrupted now and then by a period of whistling and clanking suitable for waking the dead. For a man of Uncle Oscar's sensitivity, this was the absolute bottom. His pride in his 1940 Chevrolet was gone, completely. Nor was it only the noise that made him shrink in his seat. It was the thought of being seen in a car which spewed out exhaust gases before itself as if defying the very laws of motion. It is safe to say that had there been a hole handy Uncle Oscar would have been in it.

As he approached the city, the pain of being seen in such a contraption caused him to take only side streets to avoid attention. By this time it was very late, or very early, as you would consider it. Beer gardens were refueling for tomorrow's trade, and wives on the night shift were writing notes to their husbands on the day shift reaffirming their undying love and reminding them to be sure to put out the milk bottles. Really, the only persons still about in numbers were the hotrodders who were on the side streets to avoid the cops, who were on the main streets to avoid the hotrodders.

As you might have guessed, Uncle Oscar didn't get far into town before he was spotted by the hotrodders whose eyes and ears were better than their common sense. In no time at all they were whizzing around him on all sides, their eyes bulging with curiosity. It is only natural that they would assume that Uncle Oscar was one of their fraternity, so he decided to stop, when one hotrodder drove crosswise of the road in front of him and another hooked his rear bumper, and spent half an hour turning down offers to exchange cars even up. In fact, things got so fantastic that one hotrodder offered to throw in the blonde he had with him. The only thing that saved Uncle Oscar that night was the appearance of a cop on his way home from work. The hotrodders vanished immediately. At that Uncle Oscar still had to suffer more humiliation. The cop forced him to turn around and drive in reverse so that the exhaust pipe would be in the position prescribed by law, and provided him with a siren-screaming escort home.

When Uncle Oscar backed into his garage that night his fortune was made. As soon as he could he patented the Front End Exhaust Pipe, with attachments, and sold thousands at a handsome profit. It's too bad that an inventor of his caliber, who did so much to make life worth living, had to pass on; but it provided me with a nice sum of money with which I took the trip I am telling you about.

I should tell you that Uncle Oscar was an eccentric. He was very fond of me, yet he liked my brother even more. Of course, as you would expect, this preference was reflected in his bequests; he left my brother 100 pounds of one dollar bills and he left me 100 pounds of silver dollars.

One hundred pounds of silver dollars amounts to $10,122, which you cannot disprove. Coming at this time, it was a wonderful thing, making it possible for me to take a trip. I was quite happy, that is, until I was boarding the plane to start the first leg of my trip, when a problem arose which I had not foreseen. It was significant, so I will tell you about it also.

I had planned my itinerary with great care. The first leg of my trip was to be by plane to Pongo-Pongo. In preparation I had purchased a special case in which to carry my $10,122 in silver. As I was boarding the plane at the airport, the ship's officer, noting that I sagged with the weight, demanded extra payment for the extra load. I demurred at first, then gave in to his logic that an extra hundred pounds of weight would take the place of a woman passenger, opened my new carrying case and handed him fifty silver dollars. As I again picked up my case I was struck by the loss in weight, so I demanded a refund since I no longer had one hundred pounds and the rate was by the pound. For some reason the officer showed little willingness to make the refund, arguing that no refund could be made without increasing the weight of my baggage, which would increase the cost once more, which would require more payment, which would make a refund necessary, which would increase the weight again, etc., well, right then and there I decided to make my trip by boat, so I told them what they could do with their plane and left.

Fortunately, I was able to book passage on a nice looking

boat without trouble. So I sailed with the tide, as many a globetrotter before me had done. I had a nice room on the second deck. It was the fourth day out that I first noticed that the salt air was tarnishing my silver dollars, so I went to the captain to complain. The captain, a rather small man, was very nice about it. He assured me that he would order the course of the ship changed immediately so that the sea breeze would blow from the opposite direction, and at first sight of land would have wheels put on the boat and make the rest of the trip by land. I thought that this was going quite far to please me, and was about to say so when the captain suddenly took off his cap, jammed it on my head, gave a peculiar and eerie laugh and jumped overboard. For a few moments I was upset, thinking that something I had said had been responsible for the poor man's suicide; that is, until I was told by some of the crew members that the captain just couldn't take it. Remembering what he had said about putting wheels on the boat, I decided that the man must have been crazy.

Now, I hadn't heard it myself, but persons who crowded around me at this time told me that the captain had shouted, on his way down: "Run it yourself." All seemed to assume that this remark had been directed at me, and as I was wearing the captain's cap, which he had rather roughly placed on my head at the moment of his departure, passengers and crew alike insisted that by the strange law of the sea, I was legally the captain of the ship until we reached port.

This was a nice kettle of fish. How was I, who didn't know enough about legal matters to get a Reno divorce, going to argue with them. I was captain, and that was all there was to it.

As captain, the first thing I thought to do was to move my things from the second deck to the captain's quarters. As a matter of fact, this was the only thing I did as captain that seemed at all right. From my first day I had nothing but the worst kind of trouble. The law of the sea may have said that I was captain, but I found in no time that it took more than the title to make it so.

The next morning I ordered the anchor lowered and called a meeting of all on board. At this meeting I made the statement that I would need the help of each and everyone in operating the ship. This proved to be a horrible mistake, for it was taken literally, and from that time on I was showered with suggestions of what to do and how to do it. In no time I understood why the late captain had blown his top. After three days of such torment I was on the verge of suicide myself. Late that night, clutching my hoard of silver dollars, I quietly lowered a life boat, got silently into it and rowed off into the darkness, leaving the ship with its four hundred and ninety-two captains to its fate.

The row boat phase of my trip turned out to be harrowing, to say the least which reminds me of Captain Eddie Rickenbacker's similar experience. As I drifted helplessly, for days on end, through calm and heavy seas, without sight of land in rain and sun, while the hours stretched out until each seemed an eternity, I had plenty of time to regret my rashness in leaving the ship. All I had thought to take with me was my bag of silver dollars, which was my inheritance from Uncle Oscar and now a veritable chain around my neck. I could not eat them to sate my hunger, nor drink them to slake my thirst, and in my circumstance they were not negotiable, so I used them as an anchor to slow down the pitching of the boat which was giving me saddle sores.

After five days in the rowboat I began to feel the pangs of hunger. I hadn't eaten much of a dinner before I left. It was a time to summon up all my ingenuity which I did by locating some flares in the life boat locker, out of which I fashioned a crude gun. Upping anchor, I used silver dollars for bullets, firing while lying on my back in the bottom of the boat.

You already have evidence of the care I had taken of my bag of silver dollars. Even in this situation I had no intention of squandering my wealth. I figured to pay no more than the going price of a dollar a pound for meat, nor did I intend to contribute to inflation, so when a gull flew over I loaded with a single dollar but a pelican load was three dollars fired in the same blast. With this arrangement I ate well and within my budget, but my thirst grew and grew. To satisfy this became urgent.

One day, as I hauled up the anchor, I noticed that the silver dollars were so cold that beads of moisture from the warmer air condensed on them. Seeing this as the answer to my thirst, I lowered them further, raised them, held each in-turn over my drinking cup, and caught the precious fluid as it dripped from them. Thus I was able to live through this nightmare which few would care to duplicate.

The after-effects of my ten days at sea were slight, but telling you about them will complete the picture of my suffering. One of the more annoying results was a case of silver poisoning contracted from drinking the dew formed on the silver dollars. I really was not aware that I had the disease until my nails turned silver colored. Doctors have told me since that there is no cure for this ailment so I have accepted the disfigurement as my lot in life. Of course, I had to immediately exchange my nail clippers for a bottle of silver polish.

Also, because I ate so much of the raw meat of seabirds, which are the natural enemies of fish, I have found that it is useless for me to go fishing any longer. The fish avoid any place I appear, and fish eating birds gather around me as if we were blood relatives. This is mostly embarrassing, of course.

These are the physical after-effects of my ten days in a row boat. However there were other effects of a legal and social nature which were more annoying to me. I find, for example, that my silver nails attract the wrong kind of girls, the kind who, obviously fascinated by the ends of my fingers insist on holding my hands, which limits romancing to almost nothing, as you well know.

Then there is the legal effect of my trial by sea. I can't recall whether or not I told you, but my trip ended when a fortunate breeze blew me ashore in California. After I dragged myself onto that blessed land I was met by an officer of the law who served me with a subpoena to appear in court for infringing on a patent. It seems that I had no right to shoot silver dollars as I had done. Unknown to me, the use of silver bullets was a patent of the Lone Ranger.

After paying a fine for my ignorance I decided to stay in California for a while. After all, I was a little tired--the chairs in the courtroom had been very uncomfortable. While in California I learned that silver dollars were used in the West in preference to paper dollars, so I exchanged mine, although with regret. You see, I had become very sentimental about them; then too, I looked so peculiar walking down the street with one shoulder sagging and no weight to cause it, but there are compensations for all things. I used the paper dollars that I had acquired to pad the low shoulder and felt both safe and erect.

My stay in California had its interesting aspects also. Looking around for some sort of adventure with pictures, I, one day, decided to join a nudist camp and see the world. On applying for admission, I was flatly turned down. When I asked why, they pointed to my camera and informed me that nudists were very modest people. I offered to leave my camera outside, but again met with a firm no. This time I was informed that the heavy crop of whiskers which I had grown on my sea trip prevented me from exposing all. That ended that. I was not going to shave off my luxurious growth of whiskers.

Up to now I had been spending my money as fast as my low shoulder straightened. When I suddenly realized that I sagged no longer, I was broke. Being rather old fashioned, I never thought of going on relief or collecting unemployment insurance, I just went out and looked for a job so I could replenish my dwindling finances. After considering several possibilities, I settled on motion pictures. I went to one of the big studios and applied for a job as an actor. At first they were inclined to look unfavorably on my request for a part in a picture, that is, until they spotted my silver nails and went into ecstasies of joy, explaining that I had just what the movie industry needed--something colossal, new and different. Sensing that I was making progress I took off my shoes, exposed my silver toe nails and clinched the job. I was signed to a contract on the spot and assigned to a part in a picture called "The Garden of Eden" with the understanding that I would have third billing. I was elated at my success until I learned that I had been just another victim of Hollywood trickery. When I reported for work I found that Adam got first billing, Eve second billing, and third billing was the snake.

Never one to put my name to anything I didn't intend to see through, I played the snake in the motion picture "Adam and Eve". In no time at all I began to receive fan mail in large quantities from married ladies, who, without exception, stated that I reminded them of their husbands.

I was laid up for a while after the picture due to injuries received in filming. One day my tail began itching like mad. With my arms securely encased in the snakeskin there was nothing I could to but bite the itching part with my mouth. I gave a tremendous lunge, grabbed my tail in my mouth and bit away. The relief was so great that I failed to notice that I was rolling like a hoop, down and off the stage and out into the studio lot where I came to rest against a pile of old tires and was lost for two hours.

Now it seems that under the Hollywood system, an actor's success is judged solely on the number of fan letters received, irrespective of what is said in them. As mail continued to flood in addressed to me, I was pushed into stardom by the weight of it. Adam and Eve had become a box office marvel. As is the custom in such successes, the public demanded a sequel, and since my mail outweighed that of Adam and Eve together, I demanded, and received top billing. The second picture was, therefore, called "The Return of the Snake" and featured me in three dimensions.

This picture opened as I slithered down from the apple tree and seemingly directly into the laps of the audience, as is possible in 3-D pictures. In city after city the audience reaction to this bit of film magic was the same. They left the theater en masse, precipitously, and without stopping to get their money back. This created the unheard of problem for Hollywood; a picture which was a financial success while playing to empty theaters.

The moguls of the industry huddled and discussed the impact of "The Return of the Snake" on nationwide audiences. A psychiatrist was called in for consultation and Frank Buck gave his opinion. Finally, a carefully worded statement was released to the press which explained that the reaction was mass hysteria with goose pimples.

This ended my brief but effective career in the movies. I was forced to turn in my snakeskin and was barred forever from acting in anything but television plays; however, the Actor's Guild, whose members appreciated the perfectness of my portrayal of the snake, immortalized me by adding a full length impression of my Snake characterization to the footprints of other fairly good actors at Grauman's Chinese Theater.

It was at this time that a yearning for home and friends gripped me. It was so compelling that I could no longer ignore it. I recall that I was in a restaurant at the time. My longing became so real that I fancied I was drinking some of that good Coopersville water, which made me cry so hard that I had to lay aside my limburger sandwich. It's funny how little things can take on such an air of importance when a person is longing for home.

I decided to motor home and went over to Sam's Used Car Lot for a car. Sam, who was in business only to serve the public, sold me a car at such a ridiculously low price I was almost ashamed to take it. In fact, I wouldn't have excepting that it was equipped with a Front End Exhaust, one of dear dead Uncle Oscar's inventions as you recall.

I began my trip home in a gay mood. Perhaps I was a little bit too gay, for I landed in jail before I got out of California. This time the circumstances were so unusual that they demand recounting. You may think that all this had something to do with the front end exhaust pipe, but that is not so. The law had long ago made them legal for obvious reasons. You remember the trouble Uncle Oscar had had on that score; well, when cars began to be produced in large numbers, so equipped, and purchased by law abiding citizens who willingly drove in reverse to comply with the law, the safety experts were not long in admitting that the situation was hazardous, and urged that automakers take cognizance of the peril. Loyal, to the very bottom of their pocketbooks, the auto industry began to adapt itself to the new revolution in motoring, bowed respectfully to Uncle Oscar and applied their know-how to the problem.

It proved a knotty problem, however, and things stalled while the hazard on the highways increased. The vacuum, when it was finally penetrated, occurred in a way that gives one renewed faith in the common man.

One day a note was dropped into the suggestion box in one of the larger auto plants by an employee known only as "Goofy Jones". In his unique literary style Goofy Jones had scrawled, "If their a'gonna back up all the time why in hell don't ya put the headlights on the back end?" Here at last was the answer.

After rewarding Goofy Jones with a free oil change, the company did just that. In no time a competitor moved the windshield to the rear of the car, and a style-setting automaker gambled all by moving the engine and steering wheel to the rear of all his models. It's amazing what these relatively simple changes did to make the highways safe again. The death rate on the highways dropped almost overnight from 682 per hour to a mere 600, which was considered normal.

Well, to return to my trip home I was arrested and thrown in jail as I said. It was one of those small town jails, in the rear of the engine house. The charge against me was creating a traffic hazard. The complaint was made by a woman who has had enough experience in creating traffic hazards to know one when she saw it.

This woman said that she was blinded by the reflection of the sun on my silver nails. It seemed that there was to be no respite from the suffering I had to endure because of this malady.

In jail I was the object of a great deal of small town curiosity, and when country folks from miles around began to come for a look, the enterprising jailer began to charge admission. This made me feel like a monkey in a cage. Eventually I was sentenced to pay a $25 fine and freed, but the Justice of the Peace nobly cancelled payment because the gate receipts had paid for his new office.

I had endured all this with fairly good humor, but word got around that it was financially profitable to arrest me and put me on exhibition for an admission fee, and every small town cop on my way home laid for me. You may not believe it, but on my entire trip home I paid for more civic improvements than W.P.A.

I am home again, and you have no idea how happy I am to be able to tell you about my trip. By now you know that I have traveled by that most ancient of all vehicles, the imagination, and that my pictures are all mental images conjured up in your minds as I have talked to you. Perhaps you don't consider this quite fair. If so, I am sorry, but think of my chagrin as you came and went in your travels while I stayed at home suffering humiliation and shame. At least, I can now sit among you with some degree of self-respect.

##

You "newly skinny's" have now joined with me, but we are still different, I assume that you are on a special diet of fuzz and fluff while casting a covetous eye upon any hearty eater you may encounter. I, on the other hand, eat without concern for my weight. Now, however, I am becoming worried. Every time I read an article on diet it exposes another food as harmful to health. White bread is without food value, sugar causes loss of memory, food colorings are poisonous, milk is loaded with poison, beef is full of poison. I'd pity the cannibal who got me for his dinner. Eating my flesh would be the equivalent to drinking wine with the Borgias.

1960   THE SPACE ADVENTURE

I suppose you'd call Uncle Oscar a spaceman, Actually though, he was just a bum inventor whose fame hinged on his invention of the front end exhaust pipe, which was such a success that it made him wealthy beyond all reason or right. Not satisfied to wallow in his pecuniary bliss, he kept on tinkering and it was while he was in this state of his career that he caught the fatal fever -- along with the Army, Navy, Air Force and high school science students -- and began to build a spaceship of his own.

The science of rocketry is extremely complicated, as anyone could guess. The problems of building a space ship are so enormous that only the most advanced scientists have dared to attack them. It is typical of Uncle Oscar's gigantic conceit that such knowledge failed to deter him in the least. With the model "T" approach to the problem, he set up his working area in he backyard, and over a period of time, working as the will struck him, evolved a make-shift masterpiece, no less.

When this phase of the great man's career began, Aunt Minnie was against it until she satisfied herself that Uncle Oscar was not spending an excessive amount on the project, and did not intend to take any of his fabulous earnings with him into space, when she contentedly returned to her crocheting, which vocation she pursued to retain her sanity amidst all the confusion which surrounded the household as a daily course.

As I stated previously, I suppose that Uncle Oscar could be called a spaceman, especially since he's been out there somewhere for over six months now without a word to even his closest relatives. He finished this "bloomin' contraption", took his peanut butter sandwiches, got in it, and took off successfully for the moon. This was back in the spring of the year. No one knows if he made it or failed, which keeps Aunt Minnie crocheting monotonously while the neighbors show increased interest in living their daily lives. Of course interruptions steal much of her new-found peace of mind. People telephone, or drop by regularly to report, various celestial abnormalities which they feel might have a relation to Uncle Oscar's whereabouts. A meteor cannot fall now without one or more sky watchers reporting its fiery death to Aunt Minnie.

We'll probably know one of these days what became of Uncle Oscar, and if you personally don't give a damn, the scientific world will, because his success has embarrassed them extremely. Their monstrously expensive cylinders of stainless steel seem to them now to be monuments to their ineptitude, and it is safe to say that should Uncle Oscar return from space they might conceive thoughts of harming him--severely, that is.

The family isn't proud of the fact that Uncle Oscar is a spaceman. There are problems growing out of his scientific success; for instance, when will he get back with the lawnmower motor? For income tax purposes, is he still a dependent? Must he fill out a tax return? Should he be called an absentee voter? Should the Census Bureau include him in the population? Should Aunt Minnie quit crocheting and relax?

Even Uncle Oscar's admiring nephew--just a mere lad with little understanding of relative values--met with a problem. At a regular school session his teacher asked the boy if he would invite Uncle Oscar to the P.T.A. meeting soon to be held. The nephew replied, "Uncle Oscar ain't here anymore." After correcting his grammatical lapse the teacher asked: "Where is your Uncle Oscar?" to which the boy replied: "He's up there," pointing to the zenith. Jumping to conclusions the teacher assumed an attitude of reverence such as is effected by people at the mention of the dead, and said, "so your Uncle is in heaven?" Whereupon the nephew, wanting to clear up this misimpression said, "No, he's on the moon."

This teacher was not altogether unsophisticated, but being a teacher she saw in this a learning situation which she was compelled to grasp. Taking plenty of time and care, she ignored the other twenty odd pupils in her class and used the ensuing fifteen minutes to clear up, what to her, was an horrific misunderstanding about a theological conception with the result that now the young lad is telling his friends that his Uncle Oscar missed the moon and went to heaven, as if he considered this an inglorious feat, and was engulfed in disappointment. In time rumors of this reached the preacher of the church where the boy attended Sunday School, who, fearing to have such a misimpression circulating among the youth of his congregation, used the next Sunday to preach on the topic: "Destination

Heaven, by Mistake."

Now actually, to anyone who knew Uncle Oscar, or wished to compare his earthly record with the eternal yardstick for admission to heaven, it would be obvious, to even the uncritical, that this man lacked the qualifications for admission to heaven by rocket ship or any traditional method of propulsion. He could, of course, have gone into orbit around the celestial haven, outside the three mile limit, naturally, but out of reach of the devil, to have become a sort of spaceman without a country, admittedly a fitting end for such an unorthodox character as Uncle Oscar,

The vastness of space has absorbed Uncle Oscar much like the storm sewer absorbs a drop of rain. Both are in it somewhere, but who knows where. His blast off was not entirely unwitnessed even though it was accomplished in the darkness of early morning, and the fortunate few who saw it called it a miracle of levitation. If I may say so, I would suggest that the propulsive force came less from explosives and more from the combined wishes of the neighborhood to be rid of Uncle Oscar for good and all. At any rate, the ascension had its mysterious aspects.

For the past six months the Pentagon has had the area between the garage and the west fence line under constant guard. No one but authorized personnel has been allowed to enter the area, for it was here that Uncle Oscar's space vehicle was erected and the count down must have taken place. All the high brass has viewed the scene, and F. B. I. agents are constantly lurking in the vicinity, although their jurisdiction over space matters is dubious, if not pure fancy. Wherever Uncle Oscar may be he is free of all governmental authority, which, with his attitude of rebellion, often voiced and angrily announced, would certainly mean that he will stay away as long as he can extend the nourishment in his peanut butter sandwiches.

But Uncle Oscar will be back. You can count on it. For one thing, he has an order all filled out to Sears Roebuck which was not mailed. Also, during the ascension he somehow or other dropped his lighter, and being the addict he is, you smokers understand best why. Meantime, keep your eyes open. The heavens may vomit him back to earth in your vicinity.

################################

"0" is the symbol for nothing, or zero. Zero or nothing means completely, entirely, totally without. If this be food, one is starving; if this be clothing, one is nude; if this be work, one is idle; if this be sense, one is daft; if this be gasoline, one is a pedestrian; if this be rain, there is a drought; if this be courage, one is a coward; if this be life, one is dead; but if this be money one suffers only a slight inconvenience for the Government and its citizens have both become adept at living on the negative side of zero.

################################

They jog by, they bicycle by, and I've wondered why. Now I know. The new world of electronics is doing away with physical exertion even to the extent of running to answer the telephone. Gadgets take over. One need not exercise his finger to dial the phone any longer. The human machinery is out-dated and being replaced with more efficient wires and tubes. God help us! What if one day our women find a $2995 gadget more satisfying than a bungling husband. You'd best consider such possibilities.

UNCLE OSCAR - POLITICIAN

Uncle Oscar, inventor of the front-end exhaust pipe, and more recently space man, just returned from Africa, is a fungus on our family tree. It is only honest to say that we detest him for the perpetual embarrassment and continuing disgrace he causes us, yet we can hardly let him know our true feelings toward him when we must view him through the dollar sign, so as to speak. His fortune intrudes upon our right as relatives to regard him with the odium he so richly deserves. Knowing that he will leave us the scions of wealth at his death, we have developed a willingness to endure him which we acknowledge to be purely avaricious. Our moral position is, of course, untenable--"stinky" if you wish to be exact--but there you are. You mix the blackness of your regard for the man with the green of his money, and you get the color of Erin.

Now take the space adventure which I related to you last. It caused only embarrassment. Should we be blamed for secretly hoping that Uncle Oscar was gone for good and all? I don't think so! There was a period during his absence into the unknown reaches when we came out of hiding, enjoyed life, spoke to the neighbors, received a reply which was not a curse, and behaved like rational human beings. Our dignity returned, and the smirches on our family name seemed less significant. We even forgot temporarily that we were heirs to a multitude of cruel jokes as a result of the invention of the front-end exhaust pipe, that our paternal ancestor was the anathema of the scientific world because of his model-T space ship, whose every revolution galled the creators of magnificent fizzles which fried on their own launching pads.

Well, Uncle Oscar came back to the bosom of his family. Back from Africa where his space ship landed inconspicuously in a jungle clearing. His welcome there was black; black men, that is, and these citizens of the dark continent apparently understood Uncle Oscar. Anyway, he is a life member of their tribe with all rights and privileges.

At home Uncle Oscar was hailed before a board of inquiry of the military where hostility was the tone. This was due to the lampooning they suffered because their repeated failures and Uncle Oscar's success were in such contrast. What happened hasn't been publicized, but it is known that there was a shake up in the general staff, and a Sears-Roebuck executive is now included in an advisory capacity.

Yes, Uncle Oscar is back, back in his ramshackle workshop which sprawls about the back yard, its sway-backed roof permitting glimpses of the growing piles of debris behind them. We hear again the squeek-squawk of the machinery, interspersed with the screech and whine of metal passing through them, the jarring clank of hammer on anvil, and, during the lulls, the maddening humming of Uncle Oscar himself as he contentedly works away, oblivious of all around him. Around him, and of course, around us is the oppressive atmosphere caused by the union of hope of the neighborhood that something dire will happen to take Uncle Oscar away before his time.

After Uncle Oscar amassed his great wealth, which came from the invention of the front-end exhaust pipe, and enhanced his fame by devising a successful rocket ship in which he toured outer space, his townspeople recklessly elected him a member of the village council. Uncle Oscar, buried in his dilapidated workshop from sun-up to sun-down daily, was oblivious of the fact that the campaign to make him a council man invoked tremendous discussion and separated the town into two warring camps. Those favoring his election pointed to the good he had done the community by calling it to the attention of most of the nation with his invention and space travel, and spoke unadvisedly of his talent for accomplishing the impossible, which they were certain could solve the village problems in a twinkle. Those against were mostly shrewd people who could see through all the flim-flam, or near neighbors of Uncle Oscar's who regarded the great man with contempt, spoke of him derisively and prayed for their deliverance from him without a care as to the method by which it might be accomplished.

The great man won election to the village council without shutting off a lathe, interrupting his routine, or casting a vote. Then the trouble began; he shut off his lathe, interrupted his routine and attended a council meeting. Irritable by nature, socially ignorant of the ways of the civic-minded, stubbornly sure of himself, falsely self-confident in his convictions, narrow-minded, opinionated and mouthy, he had all the earmarks of a trouble maker, which he was not long in becoming.

The resentment concerning Uncle Oscar's election to the village council showed up quickly. The unhappy members of the group lost no time in making an attempt to put him in his place. The first order of business at the opening meeting introduced by a motion was, to wit: "I move that the council enact an ordinance requiring all persons within the village limits to remove unsightly rubbish piles within thirty days or pay a fine of $100."

There may have been other unsightly rubbish piles within the village limits, but none so noticeable or more directly aimed at than those behind Uncle Oscar's work shop, which had grown and grown through the years until the neighbors children, who had been born and raised in its shadow, wrote themes in English class about the sun rising over them, as if they were the eastern limit of the world. All of the numerous complaints about these junk piles previously registered with the village council had been ignored out of deference to Uncle Oscar's wealth and fame, or out of plain cowardice generating from fear of crossing such a crusty, crotchety character. Now the ax fell with a thud, not only on Uncle Oscar's neck but also on the flowering of his political career as a town councilman.

All the fury of a March blizzard, all the noise of cascading water, all of the explosive force of escaping steam, all the roar of an avalanche would have come as the expected reaction from Uncle Oscar at this pronouncement, but startlingly enough he only raised his somewhat shaggy head and seconded the motion. The astonishment at this totally unexpected response wilted the assembled group, all of whom were tensed and braced for the expected onslaught. A stunned silence followed which Uncle Oscar didn't seem to notice, but which gave the other councilmen time to eye each other uneasily while the awkwardness of the moment increased.

Finally, the village president, remembering his function, managed to ask weakly if there was any discussion of the motion as stated. Once more in startling fashion Uncle Oscar straightened in his chair and asked that the motion be re-stated, which was done, less apprehensively this time, but the secretary had no sooner finished the reading than a great oath erupted from the lips of Uncle Oscar followed by a torrent of epithets, and a gushing of vituperation which spared no one present whether friend or foe. When this issuance had subsided to a gurgle of uncomplimentary remarks about unsightly features present in the village other than rubbish piles and dried-up with some mutterings about unfairness, the assembled council members sat as if in a stupor, silent and cowed by the unexpectedness of it all.

At that precise moment the fire siren, located on the roof of the village hall wherein the council was meeting, began screaming out its call to the volunteer fire men. From stupor to frenzy was only a brief instant. The council members, including Uncle Oscar, were on their feet in a wink as if yanked out of their chairs, scrambling to the call of the siren as all volunteer firemen do. In no time the chamber was devoid of humanity and the minds of council members were on extinguishing the fire.

This unexpected turn of events appeared, at the time, to have bailed Uncle Oscar out of a bad situation, and it did, but as events ensued it also accrued to his benefit in an unforeseen manner. The interruption resulting from the fire alarm served to cool down tempers and permitted some time for thought about the incident by the council members. The week following was one of discussion and re-consideration and out of this gradually there developed a totally unexpected and thoroughly erroneous conclusion, namely, that Uncle Oscar had "played it smart," and was an adroit politician. The reasoning went like this: as Uncle Oscar had seconded the motion himself and then blasted it on a re-reading, which he himself had demanded, he had confounded all present, obscured the issue and displayed daring tactics which were certain to result in a defeat of the motion. Consequently, when the council reconvened the great man was accepted on these terms as a respected member, and the unseconded, unvoted on motion regarding rubbish piles was not intended to be introduced again into the business of the council.

Well, the truth was....What does it matter what the truth was. The fact is that Uncle Oscar was now inventor, spaceman and politician extraordinary. Never did one man have so many undeserved successes, never was one man viewed in such a distorted mirror. Any of his relatives could have set the record straight with one mouthful of words, but no one would have listened anyway.

Installed as a respected member of the village council, Uncle Oscar began a political career that rivaled his space adventure in uniqueness. His rubbish piles unmolested, he sank into a bored attitude, and said very little about what he considered minor matters which then occupied the attention of the council. When they adopted a motion to erect more 'No Parking' signs about the village for people to ignore, Uncle Oscar suggested that they open a parking lot for cars; when they considered the problem of juvenile delinquency Uncle Oscar suggested that they erect a swimming pool, and when they discussed snow removal Uncle Oscar suggested that if the Mississippi River were reversed in its flow, it would bring the warm water from the Gulf of Mexico to the Great Lakes and make Michigan a second Florida, and besides as he said: "This country needs more room for shuffle board."

It was unique suggestions such as this one that made council meetings last longer than they normally had, and as the lights burned on in the village hall, people noticed, and concluded that the council was giving better attention to their needs. In fact, townspeople came to speak of this council as the "do something" council which both pleased and flattered its members and won them uncontested re-election. Under the circumstances, no council member dared to criticize Uncle Oscar, rather they were forced to praise him openly which galled them because they realized that besides carrying on the business of the village without his help they were also carrying Uncle Oscar along with them while he won most of the applause.

Forced to praise Uncle Oscar as a councilman, while secretly detesting him, put these gentlemen in much the same position that we were in as his relatives. There was no way to cope with the situation, save by muttering to yourself, unless you indulged in thoughts of murder. I just know that Uncle Oscar has been done away with imaginatively in a thousand ways. If all the thoughts about him became reality, he would have a tomahawk in his head, knives protruding from his anatomy like quills from a porcupine, enough lead in his system to make him a bonanza and so much poison that, could he be equipped to spray like an aerosol bomb, one could use him to exterminate all the insects on a 40-acre farm.

Thus, to get rid of Uncle Oscar was the problem. Revered and admired by those who knew him only incidentally, abhorred by those who knew him well, he was publicly wanted and privately wished away. It is no wonder that Uncle Oscar's fellow councilmen began secretly conniving to be rid of him, and so thinking, should drift quite naturally toward his relatives who had done much thinking in the same vein.

Their appeal to relatives was only wishfully met. Aunt Minnie, remembering the era of peace and quiet during Uncle Oscar's time in space, suggested feebly that he might be induced to build another space ship and again take off into the vast, unknown, but again, it was Uncle Oscar himself who resolved the dilemma. The great man was so vain and so near-sighted when it came to seeing himself as others saw him, and his entrance into politics as a village councilman looked so successful from his viewpoint, that he, noting that a national political election was in progress, decided to run for office of President of the United States.

As you must be aware this is a presidential year and a couple of guys by the names of Nixon and Kennedy are each heavily favored to win by partisan groups who have staged huge nominating conventions in their interests, but this was done without any knowledge of Uncle Oscar's political prowess or without any expectation of competition from Uncle Oscar.

I suppose until this decision was made there was very little danger that Uncle Oscar would compete in a national election, but strangely enough his name had been mentioned in certain quarters where he was known and admired, and with his decision to enter the contest, even at this late date, Nixon and Kennedy would do well to consider him serious opposition.

You see Uncle Oscar has a platform which is unbeatable in this age of international considerations and space explorations. If Eisenhower won the election because he knew about war from first-hand experience as a general of the army, Uncle Oscar knows about space, he's been there, and he has lectured on the subject, if somewhat locally, no less entertainingly, and he has numerous times unveiled plans for leading an expedition to colonize the planets. As the world's only interplanetary traveler he owns a voter appeal that is potent, and minimizes and obscures local and national issues.

There is some discussion in the nation's press about which candidate, Nixon or Kennedy, can best stand up to Krushchev of Russia. Here again Uncle Oscar leads the field. The wily Russian leader has never done verbal battle with a man of Uncle Oscar's vitriolic qualities. When Uncle Oscar denounces someone with his scathing tongue they are really scorched. Aunt Minnie is a fine example of that.

When Uncle Oscar was so long away on his space journey, and the only diversion was dodging meteors, he had ample time to concoct plans and schemes for improving the earth. In one of his first speeches,after his return to America, he advanced to an appreciative audience his scheme to put into effect an interplanetary Townsend Old Age Plan whereby each person over the age of 60 would have a monthly income of $100 derived from funds obtained from the sale of lots on the moon.

Giving further consideration to the eligibility of Uncle Oscar for the office of President of the United States, let me point out that the religious issue disappears when Uncle Oscar is considered. He just doesn't have any religion, or if he does, it is too feeble to be a factor.

Take the troublesome Congo issue. Uncle Oscar has an ace in the hole there. His tribal membership, granted when his space ship landed in that area, insures him of wide spread support in this contention that he could bring peace to the Congo in no time. "I can talk to them. I know those boys personally," he says.

Now, my friends, I am a relative of the great man, so I am prejudiced. I will not vote for him because Washington is not far enough away from home, but consider this, both Kennedy and Nixon are good strong candidates; however, if I were not a relative nor prejudiced, I would vote for Uncle Oscar. The man is simply amazing, and isn't that the sort of man we need for President? You have only until November to make up your minds.

FURTHER ADVENTURES OF UNCLE OSCAR   1967

Take it from me Uncle Oscar was always the rebel, the radical, the iconoclast. He never gave in to the conventional ways of doing things. He raised his children by remote control; they were so afraid of him that they avoided contact with him whenever possible, and the best way to avoid contact with Uncle Oscar was to mind his edicts on proper behavior and deportment scrupulously well. Out of fear of his violent wrath his children were as close to models of perfection as juveniles could ever be, which is equivalent to saying that they looked good beside the neighbor's brats.

Now one of his sons, my cousin Elmer, wishing a more intimate relationship with his father, decided to appear at Uncle Oscar's tumbled down workshop, which lay draped around the backyard of the homestead with the same disorder as a pile of paper cartons dropped from the sky by a Latter-Day superman.

The boy entered the workshop apprehensively, expecting to hear at any moment a blast of epithets sufficient to scour his ears and impel him to precipitous flight when he saw his father, Uncle Oscar, bent over a metal saw, and became aware that the sound of operation was sufficient to drown out the sound of his approach. Elmer was emboldened, and bravely, or rashly, walked up behind his busy father and tapped him on the shoulder.

Come to think of it, I can't recall ever having told you that Uncle Oscar was missing his right thumb, nor that his eldest son left home at the age of 17 with the feeling that it was in his best interest.

Uncle Oscar grieved for days after these events--30 days about his lost thumb and 1 day about his lost son. Fortunately the lost thumb came after many of the great man's outstanding achievements such as the front-end exhaust pipe and the spaceship, so was less an impairment than it seems.

When his period of mourning ended, all about him were aware of it, especially Aunt Minnie who always bore the brunt of Uncle Oscar's bad nature, and with a patience that ennobled her.

The day began with Uncle Oscar exploding with curses

reminiscent of normal days in the household and ended in the same way. His bad temper endured for days until he appeared from his workshop for supper one evening, unbelievably subdued, and willing to chat amiably about anything. It was as if he had been drunk for all these days and was suddenly sober.

As no one ever knew what touched off his wrath, no member of the family ever knew what ended it, but all speculated this time on the latter. So as they chatted around the supper table this evening, each sought the reason for the sudden amiability of their normally tyrannical father and husband.

Of course, it was Aunt Minnie who spotted it first, though its a wonder they all hadn't noticed because it was that obvious. Uncle Oscar had a new right thumb, a surprisingly good facsimile of the lost member. It was a very functional digit also. It behaved his wants almost as well as if operated by the brain through nerves and tendons.

Naturally, everyone present was curious about this last and rather miraculous achievement, even though they should have expected as much from a man of Uncle Oscar's genius. Being, as I said previously, in an amiable mood, Uncle Oscar indulged their curiosity by demonstrating various capabilities of his new right thumb, and it operated well for everything he chose to demonstrate, which extended from dealing cards to rolling a cigarette, with one exception, every time he rased his arm to brush the unruly lock of hair from his forehead--one of his oft repeated and very characteristic mannerisms--the new thumb refused to function remaining stiffly extended before his nose, leading one to believe that he was giving a familiar and affronting salute.

Well, for all that, it had to be admitted that this was the best artificial thumb ever created by man, marvellously constructed of miniaturized electronic equipment. What did it really matter that Uncle Oscar got poked in the eye occasionally, when he patented his thumb and produced a variety of right and left limbs and digits for amputees which added amazing sums of money to the great man's income, and eventually to my inheritance, which tale I told you about once.

Of course, I can't leave you wondering about Cousin Elmer's fate. I must tie up the loose ends of my narrative.

Poor Elmer left home a scared boy of seventeen having only one desire, to get as much distance as he could between himself and his thumbless father, He hitch-hiked to the city where he quickly fell into bad company as all teen-age boys do when left to their own devices. I hate to recount heart-breaking stories, but they do make one feel better with himself, don't they?

To get back to Elmer, in the city he fell in with a group of decadent adults called "Squares", who met furtively at the Y.M.C A. to preserve the status quo, and openly discussed their views on controversial subjects ranging from miniskirts to moon exploration, always from a dissenting point of view while chain smoking extra-long Benson and Hedges 100 cigarettes and drinking extra strong Yuban coffee, both intemperately. They were "way out" in their attire, dressed in outlandish styles of past generations, and flaunting short hair cuts in an apparent effort to attract attention to themselves.

This clique of anti-social reactionaries who scorned the long hair and "mod" clothing of the contemporary society, lost no time in trying to indoctrinate Elmer into their beliefs, and it's a wonder this naive boy didn't succumb to their way of thinking. Fortunately, before it was too late Elmer escaped their clutches and joined a group of normal young people who spent their time in more constructive activities such as defying parental authority, police authority, school authority and the draft, participating in civil rights demonstrations, street corner riots and advocating free love.

It was here in this setting and among this company that Aunt Minnie found him, took him back home, soothed his hurt feelings with kind words and appetizing food, and sent him to bed.

By morning Aunt Minnie felt confident enough of the rightness of her actions to announce to Uncle Oscar that his truant son was back home. On hearing this Uncle Oscar held his electronic thumb before him, eyed it for a long time, sighed as if in memory of the real thumb, and said, "Oh, well!" and that was that. Elmer was back in the bosom of his family again.

It was a strange thing about Elmer though. His stay in the city had altered him considerably. He was no longer the same meek, easily cowed boy he had been before. His brush with freedom made him a problem at home. He suddenly began to exert himself in ways that soon enough had him dominating his younger brothers and sisters and his mother, my Aunt Minnie. In due time things began to shape up for a contest of strength between Uncle Oscar, the old champion of the iron will, and the brash young challenger, Elmer. The bout only awaited the inevitable spark.

The storm struck on Mother's Day, of all times, and it was a classic of profane expression, vitriolic vituperation, and raucous railing which petrified the family with fear that it might break out into physical violence, but it didn't. The challenger proved that he was a match for his irascible parent, a true "chip off the old block", and when the argument subsided the great man looked upon his eldest son, Elmer, with grudging admiration, and from that time on treated him with respect as an adult, took him into his workshop, and in a way, laid the foundation for perpetuation of the worst of himself.

Whether unconsciously or deliberately it was never known, but the family certainly wondered when it came to light that Uncle Oscar had been secretly constructing a two-man submarine. He was such a sly, conniving old fox that it wasn't difficult to believe that he had deliberately allowed Elmer to best him in that abusive language battle in order to get the second man needed for his submarine.

All at once the family knew why Uncle Oscar had been reading about ship wrecks and sunken treasure of late. Obviously he was scheming to get his hands on some of it. His submarine proved to have an amazingly prehensile mechanical arm able to grasp even rather heavy objects from the sea bottom.

To move his ship from its land base to the sea, the great man had overhauled two helicopters purchased at bargain prices from army surplus stores. He intended to fly his sub to sea.

You've heard a lot about U.F.O's, I know, and I don't want to steal your pleasure in imagining that there are invaders from outer space, but this flying object talk all started when Uncle Oscar and his son Elmer set out to go to sea. The sight of a submarine soaring by in the sky propelled by the helicopters started such rumors, believe me.

When Uncle goes pioneering he's gone for a long time. His space travels took months as you remember. He and Elmer have been to sea now for 89 days, and no communication from either of them. Aunt Minnie has dusted off the gravestone she bought for Uncle Oscar when he was space traveling, and has had a duplicate made for Elmer. Cobwebs are growing in the workshop behind the house, and the two-faced neighbors are calling these submariners crack pots and worse, but the family knows that in time they'll return, and I guess that the F.B.I, knows it too, for they are lurking around with some kind of warrant for violation of air space and the like. However this time they have brought technical experts with them with the outright intention of benefiting from Uncle Oscar's inventive genius. This J. Edgar Hoover learns fast.

Who knows the outcome of this chapter in the life of Uncle Oscar? Will he find vast treasures under the sea? Will he abduct a mermaid? Or, will he just scare the hell out of some South Sea Islanders?

###################################

I've been reading articles on Woman's Liberation. I hope I don't spot this page with my tears of remorse for having done such a nice girl as my wife so much wrong.

Forgive me, dear; I didn't realize. My mistake was in permitting you to marry me, for in so doing it seems I opened to you a life of enslavement, of drudgery, of anonymity, of boredom, exposed you to unwanted pregnancies, and abuse.

Believe me, had I not been mislead by the propaganda of my era--all that stuff about two becoming one, sharing good and bad, the joy of family--I would have insisted that you live with me, keep your own name, pursue your own career, be financially independent, avoid having children, dine at restaurants, and go fly a kite.

Fortunately, most of your married life has been lived in happy ignorance of the fact that I'm a male chauvinist, and though being thus duped, I've heard you say: "I've been very happy," and so have I, for I love you too.

No doubt your uncles are all staid and comfortable relatives who deserve your highest respect. My Uncle Oscar by contrast is a hairy-chested, highhanded, tobacco chewing autocrat who keeps his family in constant fear of his wrath. The family, as a consequence, keeps a secure finger on his pulse, figuratively speaking, so they may predict from the tremors when the volcano will erupt, and in that way be prepared to take whatever refuge seems advisable at the time.

Since the family live their lives in fear and trembling, they are quite what you might expect them to be--an uninteresting lot. This is the reason I have been reluctant to identify them for you beyond naming Aunt Minnie, Cousin Elmer and Cousin Claramae.

Just why it is that I don't lay down my pen and end my accounts of Uncle Oscar's charades, tirades, and escapades is beyond explanation. It maybe that deep inside I am proud of the old tyrant for the prominence he has attained; since, to anyone willing to overlook his unsavory personal characteristics, there remains the inescapable fact that he has earned himself a niche in the history of inventive genius, and is enshrined in the Tinkerer's Hall of Fame at Wireville, Pennsylvania. It's true that this does not remove the dents he has put in our family escutcheon, but the money he accumulates is a consolation.

To Uncle Oscar there came the day when, without just reason and prematurely, he grew concerned about his age and possibility of dying. There was no mistaking that such thoughts occupied his mind, for he had never learned in all his years how to disguise his feelings--only how to express them loudly and offensively. It is about his behavior during this period of his life that I now wish to inform you.

Uncle Oscar, having decided that he was going to die, became morbid, and like a little boy, pouting to gain affection, walked about in gloomy silence, peering out of the corners of his eyes, as if measuring the effect of his performance on the family members. If he judged the result to be less than satisfactory, he would explode with a series of oaths, or the next time with some provocative statement intended to intimidate the long since cowed and suppliant family group. Add to that the fact that he began to speak in a lugubrious tone of voice hoping to evoke a sympathetic comment, and you have drawn the picture of a thoroughly exasperating husband and father. The worse aspect of it all was that his fears were imagined, for Uncle Oscar's health was excellent at the time.

For a man honored everywhere but in his hometown, this kind of childish behavior was nothing short of degrading, and the family tried to keep it hushed up--for Uncle Oscar's benefit they said--but actually, as much for their own. To do this was not easy, for Uncle Oscar was always contemptuous of his public, irascible by nature, and so impromptu in expression that any plan they devised was merely wasted effort.

Dear, long-suffering Aunt Minnie was worrying herself sick about her husband's new attitude; that is, if you won't be mislead by her outward appearance of unconcern, which was actually a mask for her deep concern, which showed on her face as unconcern because she knew it was best for her to appear unconcerned when she was concerned. Or to say the same thing more intelligibly; Uncle Oscar's fierce temper, bad nature and coarse language had taught her long ago never to broach a controversial subject unless she felt up to facing an argument. So Aunt Minnie crocheted while awaiting the outcome with apprehension.

Meanwhile, as days passed, Uncle Oscar seemed to lapse deeper and deeper into the miasma of despair. It made one feel nauseated to watch him perform like a dying calf, and prattle like a fool. Some days he would fail to turn on a single machine in his workshop; just sit slumped in his chair, his feet on the desk, staring through the grimy window of his office cubicle unseeingly, or reading the obituary column in the newspaper with too much care and morbid fascination.

Having no luck in provoking sympathy from the family, he progressed to attending funerals in the village regardless of whether he knew the deceased or not, but he probably reached the pinnacle of his morbidity when, one evening, he picked up the family Bible as if hefting it, for this was one of the few recognizable religious acts he engaged in during his lifetime.

A person can endure so much of this sort of behavior before exploding, and Aunt Minnie was on the verge of doing just that, and if she'd owned a shred of spunk she'd have done just that. But she didn't and Uncle Oscar's preoccupation with death continued. He was seen in the cemetery reading inscriptions on tombstones and measuring their proportions, and when Aunt Minnie found a rough draft of what could become his obituary in his pants pocket, and learned that he was building a casket in his workshop, she was prostrated with fear and alarm. The possibility that he might intend to take his own life occurred to her, so to forestall this, she had the guns and ammunition padlocked away, and removed all the poisons from the medicine cabinet in the bathroom.

Along with his gloom and depression, Uncle Oscar developed a bad case of indigestion which was most noticeable at mealtime, when his conversation, sparse as it was, was punctuated with loud belches, concerning which he never once excused himself. As a matter of fact, his whole behavior at mealtime became intolerable. He approached the table sighing and dragging his feet as if he doubted his ability to make it. And this was just the prelude to the main act, which might come immediately after he had sprinkled the pepper sauce on his fried potatoes, and usually turned out to be a monologue on some aspect of old age or death.

For instance, he discoursed on Methuselah's 969 years with derision, and declared that Methuselah, not Ananias, was the world's biggest liar.

"Why", he said, "if that joker counted my children this house wouldn't hold them." Another time he brought up Ponce-de-Leon's search for the fountain of youth, and asked: "How did an imbecile like him get his name in the history books? Tell me that!" and when no one replied he returned to his meal frustrated by his inability to start an argument to relieve his confused feelings.

At the next meal he might have his saucer of coffee poised just below his upper lip and bathing the ends of his moustache, ready to cool it with his breath, when he'd blurt out: "I can't understand why anybody would want to go to heaven! Why the place must already be over-populated with namby-pambies, W.C.T.U. presidents, and big bosomed women," after which he'd glare around the table daring anyone to contradict him, and getting no response would stalk out of the room.

Of course, it might have been a mistake to challenge him there, because Uncle Oscar had spent several months in outer space, and no one knew what he'd seen or where he'd been during that time, and the thought that he might be speaking from certain knowledge struck them forcibly.

On Sunday morning the family went to church as was their custom, and Uncle Oscar stayed home as was his custom. Normally, he might do almost anything during this period, but he usually hammered on the tin buildings or raced motors ostensibly for the purpose of aggravating his pious neighbors with whom he had had many tangles over the years about the holiness of the Sabbath, and whose protests he had throttled time and again by bellowing: "If you're so interested in keeping the sabbath, why aren't you in church?"

This particular Sunday, however, he just sat and brooded. When the family returned from church, they found him in a particularly uncivil mood. He hardly gave them time to change from their finery before he nailed Aunt Minnie with the question, "Whatever happened to Hell?"

With all the practice they'd had, the family just could not adjust to this kind of surprise attack. Aunt Minnie managed to stammer out: "What do you mean?" while the others stood by like statues.

"I mean, whatever happened to Hell? I am under the impression that the place is no longer mentioned by your preacher in his sermons. Has the fire been put out?"

Getting hold of herself momentarily, Aunt Minnie snapped out: "If you want to know, why don't you go to church and find out for yourself?" and pranced out of the room to the kitchen to prepare dinner.

We all make mistakes, and this was Aunt Minnie's Armageddon, for Uncle Oscar took the dare, and on the very next Sunday went to church. If this was a brand new experience for him, so it soon became for the preacher--poor fellow--and his congregation of worshippers, for that particular Sunday's services lasted long past the usual hour of dismissal, and consisted primarily of an unannounced dialogue between the preacher--poor fellow--and an obnoxious newcomer in the pews whose heckling and badgering tactics were anything but charitable, and every thing but christian. In fact the preacher never got his sermon under way. Actually he never quite finished reading the scriptures, for with every passage he read came an immediate loud challenge from this unholy visitor; and when the preacher, choking from rage, gave up, his congregation turned upon this newcomer, not unlike an avenging horde, and the walls and ceilings of the small edifice shook with the fulminations and recriminations that were flung back and forth like thunderbolts until the site of the battle and the occasion of the gathering were lost, and the christians were unrecognizable from the unholy visitor, in terms of behavior and utterances.

Finally a decision was reached by the resounding margin of 126 to 1, and the detested visitor was thrown out of the church bodily, without ever having signed the visitors register.

As soon as the family arrived back home a new dialogue began between the heckler and his normally timid wife, only the timid wife this time appeared to be near to frothing at the mouth from righteous indignation, and the heckler--poor fellow--was getting a demonstration of how it felt to be badgered and bullied, and, for once in his life, appeared fearful and submissive. Finally, after suffering the humiliation as long as he could, the poor fellow left for his workshop, sputtering like a tea kettle.

It was a long time before Aunt Minnie became composed, and her humiliation was so great that it was several days before she left the confines of the house. Sensing danger, Uncle Oscar remained in the safety of his workshop, sleeping on the cot he used when engaged in sustained projects, getting his meals by delivery from the house. At the middle of the week Aunt Minnie went to the parsonage to apologize. She found the occupant still in a state of shock, but like a good Christian, praying for her heathen husband, and grudgingly willing to forgive and forget while fighting suggestions from his parishioners that Uncle Oscar be drawn and quartered.

Uncle Oscar, on the other hand, never one to brood long over defeat, and now completely cleansed of his morbidity, was already busily scheming revenge, the only thing his spiteful mind could conceive of in such a circumstance. Clicking off ideas like a telegraph sounder, he sorted out the one he liked best and began concentrating on it. It wasn't wise, but he chose to challenge the preacher to public debate. The challenge was made through the newspaper and it was a mistake from the very outset. Up to this point the preacher had been forgiving, his parishioners had been controllable, and Aunt Minnie had behaved no worse than many another irate wife. After the issuance of the challenge the forces of peace on earth, good will to men shed their halos and instead of "turning the other cheek" as might have been expected, began to show a positive talent for ruthless retaliation. A barrage of rotten eggs pelted the house one night, and jeers and cat-calls permeated even to the workshop, while daily poison pen letters flooded the mail box of the besieged family.

This time Aunt Minnie was magnificent. She stormed the workshop, confronted Uncle Oscar, aimed a sharp finger at his nose and demolished his plans for a debate with a blunt ultimatum, broke the half mile record in making it to the parsonage where she pled for understanding, hinted at temporary insanity, invoked the Bill of Rights, and left with a truce when the odds favored open warfare, and was for a time under the care of a physician. Poor old, good old Aunt Minnie.

Beaten again, embarrassed at his capitulation, Uncle Oscar gradually regained his self-esteem, and began plotting revenge anew. His genius never was bent in the direction of reconciliation. During the next few days, activity in the vicinity of the workshop picked up in tempo. Deliveries were made, machines hummed, people went in and out. Among the deliveries which the curious family could recognize from the window of the house were an organ, folding chairs from the Odd Fellows Hall, paint, and flowers. Also recognizable were Justin Oldberg, who often did odd jobs for Uncle Oscar, Beulah Ordway, who sang publicly for pay, and Corrine Ingersol who played the organ at the theater.

The family hung about the window full of curiosity mixed with apprehension. In their minds the one consuming question was: "What was Uncle Oscar up to?"

"Do you think he's going to start his own church?" ventured Cousin Elmer, as he held the curtains apart for a better look.

"It could be--the organ, the chairs, and all," answered Cousin Claramae. "Oh, I wish that were all we had to worry about," she added cautiously. "But I worry about that casket being there. He wouldn't commit suicide, would he?" she asked in alarm as she drew near to Aunt Minnie for comfort, hoping for a denial.

"He won't kill himself," said Aunt Minnie positively. "He doesn't want to die; he wants to live forever, and that's the one thing that's bothering him. He's suddenly realized that he can't live forever."

"Well, then," asked Cousin Elmer, "What is he doing?"

"I don't know!" said Cousin Claramae. "And I don't know," said Aunt Minnie and they all rushed back to the window just as Corrine Ingersol accompanied by Beulah Ordway left the workshop.

Naturally you are wondering why one, or all of them, didn't go to the workshop and find out what was going on there. That's because you've forgotten that Cousin Elmer went there once unexpectedly, and Uncle Oscar lost a thumb in the machinery as a result. After that incident, they were all placed on notice not to appear at the workshop unless invited--and they hadn't been invited--yet.

The family had run their thoughts into bankruptcy trying to decipher what was going on, when the next afternoon, with the delivery of the daily newspaper, came the answer. Aunt Minnie glanced through it, suddenly emitted a chilling scream and fell into a dead faint. They carried her to the sofa and stretched her out in comfort, then turned to the paper. There it was, a front page announcement of Uncle Oscar's death.

"He went and did it," screamed Cousin Claramae. "He went and did it," and she burst in convulsive sobs. Cousin Elmer stood by with his mouth open saying nothing.

It was the next morning before this grief-stricken family were sufficiently composed to go to the workshop to view the remains. It was a somber procession with Cousin Elmer supporting his weeping mother and the younger children shepherded by Cousin Claramae. Even before they reached the workshop door, they became aware of the large sign. When they were close enough to read it, they were perplexed and uncertain what to do. The sign, printed in bold red letters, announced: "No Admittance Until 10:30 AM Sunday" "Funeral at 11:00 AM."

They tried the door and found it locked against them. So, once more, bewildered and disappointed, they returned to the house. Once there, after a long silence, Aunt Minnie shook off her reverie, and looking as if she had come to a decision, said: "I wonder!"

"Wonder what?" asked Claramae.

"The time of the funeral and all--I don't believe he is dead," she said.

"Why do you think that?" asked Cousin Elmer.

"And what's the time of the funeral got to do with it?" added Cousin Claramae.

"Eleven o'clock Sunday morning happens to be the exact time that the church service begins," said Aunt Minnie.

"What of it?" asked Elmer without making any sense out of the conversation.

"Don't you see?" she asked. "He's made believe he's dead and planned his funeral so as to interrupt church. He's trying to revenge himself on the preacher and the congregation."

"But, you're only guessing," said Claramae,

"Have you seen anything of the mortician?" asked Aunt Minnie, and as if this gave her an idea, she moved to the telephone and rang the funeral home to verify the arrangements.

"What arrangements?" asked the mortician sounding angry like morticians do when they have lost a funeral they expected to get.

"Do you mean that you are not handling my husband's funeral," asked Aunt Minnie in astonishment.

"That's what I mean!" answered the mortician in an aggrieved tone of voice as he slammed down the receiver.

"Very peculiar!" said Aunt Minnie. "Something is drastically wrong, I am positive he isn't dead at all."

Of course with no other indications, they were not sure-- not really sure; so they prepared for the funeral, and said no more about their suspicions.

Came the day of the funeral. At ten-thirty they were at the workshop door. As they were the first there, they had time to look around. There was a new partition in the long hall-like interior which separated most of the machinery from the remainder of the building. A raised platform in front of the partition, with the homemade casket prominent in the center, the organ on its right, and flowers on the left. In front of the platform were rows of chairs, obviously for the mourners. Assuming that they had the distinction of being the chief mourners, the family seated themselves in the front row and waited.

Shortly before eleven, a large contingent from the church appeared in a body and took seats behind the family, surrounding their preacher as a precaution for his safety. By eleven o'clock the chairs were filled with the curious and people were standing along the sides and in the rear. It was a capacity crowd.

The church members, still burning at low fire, could not resist aiming comments at the family in a sound volume loud enough to be overheard, but soft enough so if they were accosted they could declare the accuser to be an eavesdropper. Sample remarks were: "What's the old fool up to now?" and "Too bad he ever came back from outer space!" Aside from these snide remarks they came not otherwise armed. Death softens hate, you know.

Promptly at eleven o'clock Justin Olberg appeared on the platform, flipped a switch and disappeared from whence he came. All craned their necks in close attention, and a dead silence ensued.

Then organ music filled the room and Corrine Ingersol's theater touch became recognizable even in her rendition of well-known hymns. This was followed by two vocal selections from Beulah Ordway accompanied by Corrine Ingersol at the organ, all of which served to soften the attitude of those present, and establish a mood of reverence for the dear departed one, and so successful was it that some few actually were divorced from their true feelings and inclined toward benevolence and mercy.

Nothing followed for a few seconds, and then suddenly and loudly came the somber voice of the dear departed Uncle Oscar from the confines of the closed coffin.

"Fellow Christians, Beloved Friends and Neighbors--"

A mighty clap of thunder would not have left the onlookers more amazed and speechless. They melted in their seats as the voice continued:

"You have come to bury Oscar, not to praise him---"

More wonderment! There were sidelong glances, but no sound was uttered.

"The evil men do lives after them; the good is oft interred with their bones. And so it is with me. I repent any injury I have done you--"

At this point the voice ceased, and while Justin Oldberg was making some adjustments Elmer spoke to Aunt Minnie saying "It must be a tape-recorder in the coffin."

"Shush!" said Aunt Minnie, and all was hush again as the voice was heard once more.

"You are here to rejoice in my death," intoned the voice, "but though I know this, I can only express my love for you, and the hope that in death you can regard me in a better light."

Here Aunt Minnie boo-hooed loudly, but realizing that hers was a solo performance, subsided quickly. However, strangely enough a subtle change could be detected in the audience; if hatred could be seen escaping from the hearts of people, or heard to escape like steam from an enclosed vessel, one could verify that this very thing was happening in this very room. The voice went on in dirge-like tones:

"I died, but I have been reborn a new man, and in my new life I shall win your respect and admiration because of the love I now bear you." Bewilderment showed on the assembled faces as the voice resumed: "Fortunately, you will not need to die and enter heaven to see me as a reborn person--"

Here the casket lid flew open as if impelled by an unseen hand, and out vaulted Uncle Oscar, beaming, and with outstretched arms as if ready to receive all present into his bosom. The audience reaction could be likened to a panic, and it's lucky the doors opened outward, or there could have been a tragedy. They were gone in an instant, like a bird disappearing in the foliage, like sugar dissolving. All excepting the family members who remained in their seats as if solidified there.

The last person was hardly through the door when Uncle Oscar dropped his arms, plumped down in a chair and said, "They threw me out--now I've thrown them out," and began roaring with laughter. This revived Cousin Elmer who ran to the platform, approached his father and pumped his hand with approving vigor saying: "Boy! You really got even with them this time!"

"Do you think so?" asked his father embracing his son in a bear hug for the first time ever.

Now the workshop hums its old tune, and Aunt Minnie is restored to health, Cousin Claramae has left home, Cousin Elmer has been made a silent partner in his father's business, the preacher has left his charge for a new one many miles away, the mortician is mollified, because the reborn corpse represents future business, and the newspapers have finished a series of articles on false announcements, accompanied by an apology to its readers.

The reborn Christian is heathen again, and fully as irreverent as ever. No church member ever doubts any longer that Uncle Oscar is the Devil's Disciple, and if you ask any one of them they will tell you, without hesitation, where he is going, if and when he actually dies.

###############################

The more that people have, the more, independent they become. Conversely, the less they have, the more dependent they are. The scramble for affluence and independence is one we all have, or are, participating in. Merchants know this, and cater to our desires and whims. Manufacturers know this and produce intriguing products to whet our appetites further. Eventually we become their willing victims, and in our thirst for one of everything, we spend our incomes before we have earned them. Our governments do likewise, and there we can see the error of it. Farsightedness is our affliction.

LIFE'S UPS AND DOWNS   1978

A family quarrel is a private matter, or would be if it didn't become loud enough to enjoin the neighbors. I am about to share with you, confidentially, of course, and with full reliance upon your discretion, such a quarrel. Please respect this confidence as if I possessed your signed affidavit to secrecy.

It was perhaps a year or so after his funeral--you'll recall that tempestuous occasion--when Aunt Minnie, one day, reminded Uncle Oscar that it was their twenty-fifth wedding anniversary, which caught him by surprise and caused him to recall the year of their wedding so he could compute for himself the length of time--he didn't trust women with figures. Finding that she was correct he made the usual male observation: "It seems twice that long."

She, doing the breakfast dishes, expecting nothing better from him, ignored the comment, but added that this would be their silver wedding anniversary, and spunkily declared that she expected it to be observed accordingly.

"Where do you women get such fancy ideas?" he growled, knowing his pocketbook was involved here. "Who decided that twenty-five years of marriage entitles a woman to silver? In my way of thinking it entitles the husband to a medal."

Women have bad days, and Aunt Minnie was enjoying one such. Her mood, which had been challenging, now became, in an instant, martial. With little regard for the consequences she let fly with a plate at the head of her aggravating husband, which he managed to duck, and which smashed against the kitchen wall showering him with its fragments. It being a reflex action, and definitely not in character, Aunt Minnie was instantly repentant, and expressed regret in a torrent of words, dusting off her husband's clothing with vigorous swipes of a dishtowel all the while.

"I'm sorry! I'm sorry!" she repeated as she wielded the towel up and down until an unlucky swat caught Uncle Oscar in the eye whereupon he sprang to his feet rubbing the offended member with one hand while he fended off more expected blows with the other.

Hurt and angry, Uncle Oscar grabbed the dishtowel from Aunt Minnie's hands, threw it on the floor, stomped on it, and shouted: "Egad, woman! If you want to do away with me use a gun! What ails you?"

"I'm sorry," replied Aunt Minnie, considerably ashamed of herself as she bent to retrieve the dish towel from the floor, but Uncle Oscar quickly planted a foot upon it and said defensively: "Leave your weapon where it is-I'm unarmed." But she was pulling on the towel as he held down a corner of it with his foot, and when she couldn't free it, she gave it an angry jerk, pulling Uncle Oscar's foot from under him causing him to fall backward on the floor where he banged his head against a chair leg, and, uttering oaths more fitting for a barroom, jumped to his feet holding his head in both arms while backing away from his wife in fear of what might come next.

"Are you trying to knock my brains out?" was his remark as he retreated another step or two and added: "You belong in a padded cell--you've gone mad!"

Now somewhat frightened, thoroughly penitent, obviously remorseful for having caused injury to her husband, Aunt Minnie advanced upon him with arms outstretched intending to embrace him and ask his pardon, but he, misjudging her intention, backed up swiftly as if to avoid her onslaught, stumbled over a footstool and fell heavily once more, only this time his head thumped against the china closet with great force, emptying its contents upon him with a wild clatter of smashing chinaware, peppering him with a shower of bits and pieces. Paralyzed by fear, emotionally overcome by the swiftness of events, Aunt Minnie fell to the floor in a dead faint, and there they both lay, completely unconscious in a kitchen that looked to be the scene of an earthquake; a sort of bonanza for an E unit.

Into this fearful scene, coming home for a visit after a month's absence, tripped Cousin Claramae, happy at the thought of again conversing with her mother and ready to offer congratulations on the approaching silver wedding anniversary. Entering the house as one who belonged there, omitting to knock on the door, totally unprepared for the alarming scene she was to encounter, misinterpreting what she saw as death and destruction, she quickly measured her length on the linoleum-covered floor, also in a dead faint.

She was only nicely positioned amid the wild scene of

broken dishes and inert bodies when Cousin Elmer came bounding into the house from the workshop where he had been awaiting his father's presence before starting work for the day. His punctual father failed to appear as usual, he had it in mind to determine why.

Perhaps it is time for me to bring Cousin Elmer into better focus, I have never described him to you, and he is an interesting person for a variety of inconsequential reasons, and because of a variety of disparaging personal characteristics; to wit: he is short in stature, rotund, short-legged, short-armed, short-necked, and noticeably short of mental ability. Now a partner in his father's business enterprise, he was there proving himself short of skill around machinery, and because of this, already short one finger, lucky not to be short more of them, and daily shortening Uncle Oscar's temper. He had been brow-beaten and over-awed all his life by his famous father who had only recently accepted him as his bonafide son. He had grown up to be a sycophantic drudge on whom the scars of mistreatment--more psychological than physical--showed mostly as personality drawbacks. His round head sat on his short neck like a teed-up golf ball, his face was a snowstorm of teeth, that when he smiled, obscured his pug nose. His ears were small but prominently cup-shaped, just right for catching all the abuse flung at him by his irascible father. This was Cousin Elmer.

Barging in on this alarming scene, he wilted for a moment; then calling out names, began shaking each prostrate member of his family in turn. Eliciting nothing more than a slight moan from his sister, Claramae, he rushed to the tap, drew water, and splashed some on her face immediately reviving her. Together they restored Aunt Minnie to consciousness, but Uncle Oscar failed to respond to similar administrations. Alarmed, they decided that a doctor's attention was called for, and Elmer phoned Dr. Cilly, the family physician.

It being early in the day, before any respectable physician held office hours or even considered the practice of medicine possible, he was tending his hybrid flowers when called to the telephone. "Yes, what is it?" he inquired peevishly. When told, he, to the everlasting credit of his profession, dashed to the aid of Uncle Oscar, a half block at most, and after a cursory examination pronounced him to be seriously hurt, probably a brain concussion, ordered an ambulance to transport him to the hospital, and returned to his hobby after informing his gossipy wife that "The old grouch down the block had busted his cranium."

A flurry of activity at the hospital, and Uncle Oscar was revived, but the blow to the head had caused a personality alteration in the heretofore bad-tempered, foul-mouthed, bile-spewing ingrate. Restored to his senses, he looked about in amazement, inquired of the nurse where he was, why he was where he was, and this done in a most pleasant and affable manner, light years away from his normally disagreeable exasperating mode of treating people. Of course, one instance is hardly enough on which to base a conclusion, but it appeared, for the time being, that Uncle Oscar was a changed man--for the better--and there are those persons in his neighborhood, who hearing this report, callously stated that, had they known earlier that a bang on the head would have altered his personality for the better, would have been most willing to have filled that prescription years ago.

Aunt Minnie was his first visitor, as a good wife should be, especially if she happens to be responsible for him being there. Directed into Room 351 by a nurse, she bent over and planted a warm kiss on his rough cheek. Lying in bed, facing away from Aunt Minnie, thus awakened, definitely groggy from his concussion, Uncle Oscar opened his eyes, saw a lovely young nurse on the opposite side of the bed from Aunt Minnie, assumed the kiss had come from her, and not aware of the presence of his wife, rose up, grasped the nurse in his arms, drew her to him and planted a smacking kiss on her lips. Embarrassed beyond words, the nurse ran from the room. As Uncle Oscar followed her flight with a bewildered look, his eyes came in contact with those of Aunt Minnie which were adjusted to bore holes in oak.

"Oh!" exclaimed Uncle Oscar, thoroughly flustered, "I didn't know you were here," and as a precautionary measure added: "My Dear".

"I should think so!" said Aunt Minnie in a huff, and was about to add certain vigorous opinions of such going's on when the doctor sailed into the room as doctors sail when making their rounds, which prevented this.

"You're the wife, I take it" said the doctor, introducing himself. "Your husband has suffered a bad bump on his head, but he is coming along fine," this as he applied his stethoscope to the ailing one's chest and took his pulse to the ticks of a wristwatch. "I hope you didn't hit him," he added with a professional chuckle intended to identify the statement as humor. Recalling that she was responsible for her husband's presence in the hospital, Aunt Minnie was, in a second, the picture of the concerned wife.

Having finished his examination of the patient by checking the bandages swathing his head, the swift moving doctor took Aunt Minnie by the arm and led her from the room, whispering that he wished to talk to her privately, which he did in the corridor.

"I must tell you," he said hurriedly, "that your husband has a severe head injury, severe enough so that I cannot yet be certain that he will not suffer a permanent alteration in his character."

"You mean brain damage?" asked Aunt Minnie with a dreadfully worried look on her face.

"That's possible; I cannot rule it out," answered the doctor, "he must not be excited or upset during this period of his convalescence, nor should you be unduly upset by anything he may say or do while he is like he is." With this he sped off, leaving her standing in the vacuum his departure created.

As you know, a man must be in a dire plight before his wife will condone his kissing another woman. The fleet doctor had strait-jacketed Aunt Minnie by his advice, figuratively speaking, and left her to struggle with her womanly feelings and to nurse her injured pride in this unfair predicament. Having wived the inconsiderate, intemperate, exasperating, unpredictable Oscar for twenty-five years with almost uninterrupted humility and submission, now her normal pose was prescribed to her by a doctor just when she was finding it unsuitable for the circumstances in Room 351.

There was nothing in the history of the marriage relationship of Uncle Oscar and Aunt Minnie that could possibly suggest the existence of jealousy, but human nature is without predictability. Proof of this statement, if needed, is apparent when I reveal to you that Aunt Minnie was soon immersed in a flood of jealous feelings indicating that there was still a breath of romance in her gentle heart after twenty-five years of storm and blow. She loved the old coot in spite of all.

Jealousy became a constricting snake-of-a-feeling that squeezed reason into the background. Back home, thus overwhelmed, she paced the floor nervously, imagining that her trifling husband was kissing nurse after nurse with a frequency that revealed her confused state of mind. Finally, as if reaching a decision, she donned her hat and coat and walked briskly to the hospital. Seeing the doctor on entering, she all but derailed him as he sped toward her on his way to who knows where, announced peremptorily that she was taking over the duty of nursing her husband to the exclusion of all other nurses. This so surprised the doctor and so upset his computer-like performance that he actually sat down in a nearby chair to gather his wits, and began expounding a long list of hospital regulations, county, state and national that prohibited such a thing, all of which were blunted by the rock-hard determination of Aunt Minnie. So he left her standing, and fled the scene to report this flouting of the rules to hospital authorities.

Emboldened by having won a round against the doctor, Aunt Minnie entered Room 351 where the day nurse was casually changing the bed linen, and intermittently displaying an interesting expanse of white-stockinged leg for the admiration of Uncle Oscar as he sat in a chair ogling every inch of it and leering in appreciation.

Not exactly fleeing from the room, yet somehow arriving in the corridor with bumps and bruises she didn't have beforehand, shaken beyond words and sitting on the floor watching the swinging door, the pretty young nurse made it to a standing position with some difficulty with her mind firmly made up that the interloper in Room 351 was a maniac, no less. Also she adjusted her rumpled clothing, regained her poise, and soothed her smarts, she found herself suddenly surrounded by hospital personnel who were there in response to the doctor's alarm, prepared to oust the invading lunatic he had described to them.

As for Aunt Minnie, inside the room, during this brief interval, she had completed changing the bed linen without evoking a single leer from her husband, had restored her husband to the comfort of its sheets; whereupon he, in his befuddled condition of mind, had rewarded her efforts with a resounding smack as if it were now his custom to so oblige those tending him. Holding back a strong urge to slap his bandaged face, Aunt Minnie took her seat at his head prepared to tend his needs.

About this time the assemblage in the corridor was organized and disciplined for an invasion of the fortress held presently by the demented, but sturdy, wife of the patient. The capture procedure was spearheaded by no less a person than the hospital director himself, a small, round, bald man who had armed himself by donning his eyeglasses which he considered a deterrent to violence greater in worth than size and muscle. At a signal from him the half-dozen or so burst into Room 351 with the force of a hurricane. Unfortunately, Aunt Minnie had tossed the soiled bed linen in a pile in front of the doors, and when the manager promptly wound his feet in them falling heavily to the floor, the brigade behind him dropped head-long over and upon him with a violence that all but squashed him, broke his glasses, cut his face, knocked the wind from him and altered his rotundity. Caught by surprise, overcome with terror, Aunt Minnie filled the room with shrieks that would do justice to a mad woman, grabbed a bedpan, jumped upon a chair, and stood in a threatening pose facing the pile of bodies. The courage of the invaders melted in the face of this behavior and the room was cleared of them in a twinkling, as if it were a movie scene and the projector were run backwards.

When the doors finally ceased swinging, Aunt Minnie stopped screaming, descended to the floor and regained her poise. Uncle Oscar was under the bed in a delirious state, and the hospital manager was unconscious on the floor smothered in bed linen. Quickly Aunt Minnie advanced on him, still brandishing the bed pan. Realizing that he was in no condition to threaten her, Aunt Minnie dropped the bed pan, picked up the manager's legs, and using his head as a ram, pushed him into the corridor on his stomach as if he were a wheelbarrow. She threw the bed linen out after him, got Uncle Oscar back in bed and quieted down.

Meanwhile the scattered brigade had reassembled at the far end of the corridor. They were now fully convinced that the woman in 351 was a maniac of prodigious strength, and had just agreed upon it when their leader came scooting out into the hallway on his stomach shrouded in linen. When brave enough, they retrieved him and delivered him to a doctor's care where he soon revived, and doughty as he was, returned with patches and dressings to his wounds to again take over leadership of the eviction party.

Now, by tacit agreement, the decision had been reached that the mad woman must be captured by deception rather than force. The hospital psychologist, called in for consultation, warned of the super strength of the insane, and proposed that she be lured into the corridor where a net set previously above the doorway could be dropped upon her making it easy to subdue her. But a nurse voiced a strong objection to the procedure, saying that it would be treating her as an animal, "which she is, being mad," argued the psychologist. "But she is a woman after all," replied the nurse in defence of her sex, and perhaps inferring that if it were a man this method of capture would be entirely appropriate.

"What do you suggest then?" asked the piqued psychologist.

"Since she is a woman she will respond to tenderness like any female," she answered. If there were any objections to this statement among the men in the group, they were unvoiced, although thoughts of wives who deviated from this attitude may have entered some heads.

As if her decision were everyone's decision, the nurse stated that she would enter the room herself, alone, and with tenderness, reduce the tigress to a lamb, and before anyone, including the wounded manager, could object, the nurse was down the corridor and entering Room 351. Her protection being primary in his mind, forgetting his hurts, the manager bolted after her and moving as fast as he could in his bruised condition, made for the door of Room 351 to aid his subordinate in what he felt keenly was her peril.

In the meantime, the nurse had entered the room easily enough, found hunt Minnie seated by the bed holding Uncle Oscar's hand as he rested. Fearfully she approached the assumed-to-be mad woman, losing courage with each step as the performance of her good intent exceeded the contemplation of it. When Aunt Minnie became aware of her approach, she arose suddenly with the bed pan upraised in a defensive posture; it was sufficient to throw the nurse into panic, and she turned and ran heedlessly for the doors, arriving there at exactly the same instant that the hospital manager was making his waddling entrance. The thrust of his rescue charge was sufficient to propel the slender nurse spinning backward toward Uncle Oscar's bed upon which she fell headlong, rousing him. He quickly availed himself of the opportunity, embraced and kissed her; instantly the bedpan descended upon her derriere with a wham, she shrieked, Aunt Minnie shrieked, Uncle Oscar giggled, and the nurse exploded out of the room where she joined the dazed manager who was seated on the corridor floor holding his throbbing head in his hands.

This was enough for the hospital manager. Help came and he was raised to his feet, whereupon he made straight for the telephone and called the police. "This is an emergency," he said through puffed lips, "we have a crazy woman here in General Hospital. Send enough help to subdue her and get her out of here!"

A four man detachment was sent, armed and prepared for action. They entered Room 351, and took away a docile Aunt Minnie in handcuffs, flanked on all sides by uniforms, and lodged her in the city jail, charged with as many crimes as the puffy-lipped hospital manager could think to accuse her of--and that was a long list.

My, oh, my! Who could have perceived such a conglomeration of mistakes, misfortunes, and misadventures? What a 25th wedding anniversary! What a contradiction of normal events. Could it ever be unraveled? Well, it took time, but it was--and in this manner.

Aunt Minnie was discharged from jail after a psychiatric examination proved her sane and following a stern lecture by the judge, the hospital manager recovered bearing a few scars as mementoes of his experience, the nurse revised her ideas about the innate gentleness of women, and the fleet doctor adopted the custom of applying brakes at each room door and peering in before accelerating to the performance of his duties inside. Uncle Oscar was long in mending, but his ruptured skull finally drew back together around a bruised brain that gradually lost the notion that all nurses were to be kissed. Day by day, inch by inch, and growl by growl he returned to his old temperament until one day he was entirely free of any and all symptoms of compatibility, and the family, acting as his physician, pronounced him fully recovered.

However, recovery meant a slow return of memory. The injured brain began re-playing the events of the morning of disaster, and one day the memory of the 25th wedding anniversary trickled through the fog that clouded his remembrance.

Perhaps he was changed, perhaps the blow to his head had left a permanent alteration in his attitude. Whatever it was, he felt remorse--just a tiny bit of remorse--about his remarks of that morning and his unfeeling comments concerning the silver wedding anniversary. Day by day this feeling grew in him like an inflating balloon until he felt impelled to square the account and to acknowledge that there was a shred of gratitude in his ornery soul toward his deserving wife.

Deciding on the spot that he must out-do himself to rectify his wrong attitude toward her, he set his thoughts on what he could do. One day, on business trip to New Mexico, he visited an abandoned silver mine, and learning it was for sale, bought it for the price of the land. He, with Elmer's help, spent two months sifting, through the tailings until they uncovered an amount of silver sufficient to make a sizeable plaque. This he imbedded in a piece of black walnut, highly polished and artfully designed, and engraved with the following endearing sentiment:

TO MY DEAR WIFE
IN REMEMBRANCE OF
OUR 25TH WEDDING ANNIVERSARY
THE DAY I FELL FOR YOU--TWICE

Slyly he arranged to make the presentation in the presence of all those who figured in the distasteful affair: Claramae, Elmer, the chagrined nurse, the fleet doctor, the battered hospital manager, the reassuring psychiatrist, the four policemen, and the stern judge. Before this assemblage, with Aunt Minnie tastefully gowned for a supposed party at the Workshop, he presented it to his surprised mate.

Oh, yes, I forgot to mention that he made the presentation with a wary eye to his personal safety--while lying flat on his back.

###################

Marriage tied me to a wonderful woman, someone to love and admire. Now that the afflictions of age are upon her, it is so difficult for me to accept this deterioration as deserved and adjust to it.

The latest of her incapacities happens to concern an unmistakable loss of vocal power. Whereas formerly, my dear old gal could be heard above the din of a children's party; now, like a monk mumbling prayers, she is barely audible at arms length. Such feeble attempts to be heard leave me guessing what it is she wishes to communicate, and problems result. Why it was just yesterday that she sent me to the store for envelopes, and I, misunderstanding, returned with cantaloupes. And it couldn't be more than a week since I mistook a bawling-out for a compliment, and kissed her in appreciation.

I try to be careful not to upset her. Still, because she can no longer speak up, I am obliged to ask her to repeat and repeat. This exasperates her, sets her eyes to snapping, sharpens her tongue, but restores her voice volume temporarily.

How I bewail these disrupting circumstances, marring our otherwise blissful relationship. Certainly you, being a person of good sense, can appreciate my dilemma, can't you?

Speak up, will you! What did you say?

THE BIG BUST

The regenerated Uncle Oscar was small improvement over the old. He growled, he cursed, he stepped on people's feelings, he bullied and badgered his simpleminded son, and he continued to drive his neighbors to exasperation. One change, and one only, was apparent; he now treated Aunt Minnie with new respect, and never again did he demean her, at least not in her presence. He'd learned a lesson never to be forgotten on their 25th wedding anniversary. Otherwise, all was as it was.

When it was as it was, Uncle Oscar's fertile mind conceived, and his mechanical skills created monumental contributions for the good of mankind--backwards, his critics contend--the correctness of which opinion still remains in the limbo of indecision, awaiting the test of time. Certainly a fair and unbiased judgment would never be rendered while our inventor lived, for his contemporaries just could not dissociate the man from his invention, and detestation was his universal regard among them.

Now you know as well as I that inventive genius has no heavenly guarantee to appear only in the bodies of agreeable persons. In fact, the opposite is more likely to be the case; for the grinding, exhausting mental processes that fire the mind into new and untrod avenues of thought and endeavor are hardly designed to soothe one's nervous system.

But to get to the subject, our recalcitrant relative, now restored in mind, once again began tuning the fine mechanism of his brain along the channels that had given birth to previous inventions and discoveries. Ideas stalked through his grey matter hour after hour to be considered and abandoned until great heaps of invisible discards all but engulfed his workshop office, the kitchen floor, the bedroom on his side of the bed, and were even scattered like litter along the path between the house and the workshop. A sorting process was going on that would continue until the right idea, the one that intrigued his fancy, the one that he could cultivate with detail, water with plans, radiate with the sunshine of possibility emerged. Only then would activity begin in the workshop, only then would Elmer's cup-shaped ears get a scour of criticism for less than perfect rendition of pieces and parts, only then would acute indigestion visit the inventor, and only then would Aunt Minnie return to crocheting, which to her had a sedative effect.

As I begin this chapter of one of our "unknownest" inventors, all these preludes had passed. In case you are interested, among the heaps of invisible discards lay such dandy ideas as a statue to himself, a camera to photograph U.F.O's, and a plan for a bulldozer capable of moving the North American continent 10° south opening millions of frozen acres of farmland to cultivation.

And from among such a selection, what idea did he choose: Well, after measuring it by the dozen yardsticks of possibility, practicality, utility, etc., he settled upon the rather prosaic one of saving the automobile, the energy crisis being then of paramount concern. "I can do it," he said to Elmer with a modesty that was natural to him, and in a tone of voice that was meant to hurl a challenge at General Motors, Ford and Chrysler, who, as you know, were struggling to do the same with only limited success.

Of course, saving the automobile presented entirely different problems to these giants of the industry and to Uncle Oscar. It was a case of pitting unlimited resources against unlimited genius, of sprawling factory complexes versus the workshop, of college-trained engineers versus Cousin Elmer, of a stockpile of parts and materials versus the Sears-Roebuck catalogue. With odds like these, you would bet against Uncle Oscar, I know, being the born losers that you are.

Wasting no time with trivialities such as reducing weight or stealing space from interiors, Uncle Oscar went straight to the heart of the problem, which he sensed was fuel. "Find a new fuel, a cheap fuel, a plentiful fuel," he said, "and all else will dwindle into insignificance." So he immediately began to dabble with the chemistry of explosive mixtures. He mixed, he combined, he compounded, and after months of experimentation found it--the ideal combination--new, cheap and plentiful. In celebration of the discovery he embraced Elmer, his son, and danced a jig with him among the rows of machinery in the workshop, which he never would have done for any lesser discovery, it being completely uncharacteristic of the man. The discovery came as no surprise to me; I bet on him. Genius is like that!

Now let me strain your impatience to know. I must pause here to pay homage to the discoverer, the man, the human being, to Uncle Oscar. I just know that had he made his sensational discovery as an employee of some splendidly equipped laboratory in some major city he would have attracted immediate attention from the media, and been boosted into the limelight of publicity of the sort that smother a person in glorious wining, dining, of the sort that quotes them, idolizes them, honors them in song, photographs them, patronizes them, enriches them, and puts them in an early grave. I feel that my Uncle deserved as much, but living in a small village, what did he get in its place. He was hooted at, down-graded, minimized, discounted as nothing but a tinkerer by people who had forgotten Henry Ford. The local weekly paper branded him a charlatan, his discovery a hoax, and made other libelous statements about him to which his townspeople added their approval by buying every copy. He would face the rankest kind of opposition, locally, this was a certain fact.

Only in my estimation was he accorded the honor he deserved, and then only in imagination, where I fancied seeing him clad in a toga, being crowned with a laurel wreath by vestal virgins, in the presence of the Roman Senators in a huge amphitheater over-flowing with toga-clad admirers, and acknowledging their plaudits with a bashful smile on his lips and by a slight wave of the hand. How appropriate, I thought, and then being awakened from this day-dream-how ridiculous.

Facing scorn and ridicule was an old story to Uncle Oscar; I am loathe to admit that there was an element of justice in it. I suppose that if I had been, like his townsfolk were, subjected to a seemingly endless barrage of explosions over months of time as he conducted his tests with an endless number of concoctions, I, like they, might have tossed some scurrilous comments his way. And the big explosion, the one that announced success, the one that set Uncle Oscar and Elmer to dancing, the one that sent the roof of the workshop sailing menacingly over the village scattering its portions upon the landscape, I suppose, had I been one of them, after climbing to my feet and righting my furniture, I might have been upset too; and more so if I were aware that all my epithets, all my verbal abuse were wasted, having fallen on deaf ears, rendered so by the very explosions that provoked them.

Back now to the new super-fuel. Uncle Oscar's timing could not have been better, what with the fuel crisis worrying everyone, and experimenting going on with wind and solar power, and only satisfactory in a small way. Consider the ideal qualities of the discovery of Nurin (spelled N-U-R-I-N) discovered by Uncle Oscar, and so named by him to hide from the public actual knowledge of its ingredients.

And what were the ingredients of Nurin? Since the formula is no longer secret, I will tell you. Nurin is prepared by uniting exact quantities of nuclear waste and urine. That's right! And after you have your laugh, consider the ideality of the mixture. Nuclear wastes are produced daily in growing quantities by utility companies who are having trouble disposing of them. Urine has never been a saleable commodity to the best of my knowledge (at least I have never bought any) and it is being generated from minute to minute in all quarters of the globe, and in quantities that if gathered would form rivers. Now you understand why I have called Nurin the ideal fuel. At the present moment its ingredients are free of cost and plentiful, making it the best answer to the energy crisis one can conceive of. And to this discovery Uncle Oscar held the key. A mixture of nuclear wastes and urine is not explosive unless a miracle ingredient, which only Uncle Oscar knew about, was added. Because you are trustworthy I'll tell you what the "x" ingredient was. It was a certain, exact amount of onion juice, also plentiful and cheap.

Now you are wondering how Uncle Oscar hit upon this unusual concoction. I'll tell you that also. He had been experimenting with nuclear wastes and onion juice and one day set a pan of it on the workshop floor while he ran to chase the neighbor's dog from the building, but the dog bent his leg and supplied the missing factor before being run out. In chasing it away Uncle Oscar knocked over a hot soldering iron which fell into the pan, exploding the mixture. Eureka--he had the long sought fuel.

Having discovered the super-fuel, Uncle Oscar was confronted with the problem of adjusting its extraordinary explosive force for use in automobiles. Using it in cars equipped with conventional carburetors would certainly demolish the car and put its occupants in dire jeopardy of their lives. An entirely new carburetor that would dispense infinitesimal quantities of Nurin was called for, and Uncle Oscar, using a microscope, designed such a one. It was Cousin Elmer's job to machine the parts which he did in the face of much too much unnecessary criticism from his father. The new carburetor was so designed that it could be easily installed in a few minutes in place of the present one by any simple-minded mechanic--the most numerous kind, that is.

The first test run was made using Uncle Oscar's Model A. It produced astonishing results. Besides giving a smoother, quieter running performance it produced exhaust gases that had an inoffensive smell--like an empty Masonic Hall after a pedro party--and definitely not polluting. What a boon to society this could be, and entirely unanticipated by the inventor.

Still more surprising was the mileage it gave. On a fast trip to Pandemonium, Arkansas and back, the Model A used only five gallons of Nurin which averages out to better than 90 miles per gallon. Incredible! Simply incredible! Would the ideality of this fuel have no counterbalance?

When news of this fantastic mileage circulated in Shadyville, all--even those who had sworn never to speak to the hated inventor--clamored for the privilege of having their cars fitted out so they could use it, and Uncle Oscar and Elmer obliged as fast as they could equip them. In addition, he sold them Nurin for half the price of gasoline, which good deed unfortunately did nothing about changing their private opinion of him. In fact, down at the General Store where loafers met daily in their loose, unorganized discussion group, his reputation was at this time suffering more blackening. Eventually this group got around to speculating about the use of Nurin in cars which was the big topic these days.

"Mind what I say," said one authoritatively, "them power companies will soon be sellin' their nu'clar wastes by the quart at high prices while they go on raisin' our 'lectric rate just the same."

"Yea," chimed in a grizzled lounger, "greed is where their heart is supposed to be. An' they ain't half as greedy as them oil companies. My guess is that they'll soon run pipelines into every sewage pond in the country, and drain 'em all as dry as a bone."

"That old buzzard started somethin' with his latest invention," said a third, "Why, I can see them oil companies building privies on every corner to collect urine and puttin' big neon signs on 'em invitin' the public to use 'em free."

"Right," said another, "but its gonna affect people too. Some dumbbells are gonna drink water until they bust tryin' to become sorta human oil wells. An' them young mothers; I can see them wringin' diapers for every drop, and whippin' their kids for using the neighbors' bathroom instead of their own."

"You ain't kiddin'," responded the grizzled lounger, "and I'll bet ya them Indians over there in India will all stand up to a big tank an' sell directly."

"An' them Roosians and Chinks too," contributed another. "They're all full of it. Water's what they live on mostly I've heard tell," he added knowingly.

"Did ya' hear what happened at the Old Settler's Picnic last Tuesday?" interjected a tobacco-chewing farmer. "Somebody took the Men's and Women's signs off the toilets at the park and put up Shell and Gulf emblems in their place."

"I'll say this," said the oldest man present, "I feel sick when I think of all that stuff I've wasted in my lifetime. If I'd a bottled it and kept it, I coulda started my own company."

"It jus' ain't natural," said a new voice. "It's like draining people to fill gas tanks. We wan't made for that to my way o' thin'kin'. The bible says---"

Here he was interrupted by his young son pulling on his sleeve and pleading "Daddy, I've got to go to the bathroom." The father arose from his chair, took his son by the hand, and after a few steps turned back to the group and said, facetiously: "I think I'll have the kid sell to Standard Oil," departing amid guffaws.

Such ridicule did nothing to harm the prospects of Nurin as the ideal answer to the energy crisis, nor did the disparagement of its inventor harm its future.

Uncle Oscar now had the Arabs on the ropes. They hastily conferred, flew a delegation to Shadyville, offered vast sums of money, 100 camels, 2000 wives, and the Great Pyramid, to have the formula for Nurin suppressed, and left crushed and bewildered when Uncle Oscar declined. The Russians sent spies to steal the formula, but they were trained to enter marble buildings and rifle storage cabinets and couldn't penetrate Uncle Oscar's workshop. They only barked their shins and tore their clothing in the junk-filled yard. The F.B.I. and the C.I.A sent agents who ended up exchanging pistol shots and left.

With local people using Nurin as a fuel in increasing numbers, a strange thing occurred. All of a sudden, lawns in the vicinity began to grow at a rate that required daily mowing, the weeds in vacant lots grew to such heights, and were borne up by stems and stalks of such sturdiness, that children got lost in them on the way home from school. Hordes of insects arose out of them at nightfall to descend on slapping and cursing citizens. On nearby farms the crops flourished with such luxuriance that the harvesting of them kept farmers up nights and lowered the birth rate. With the townspeople unhappy and the farmers, joyful, feuding resulted. Finally an expert was sent to the area by the State. In two weeks he discovered the cause - Nurin. "The exhaust gases," he said, "rising in the air were brought down by rain and dew as a most potent fertilizer. This caused the rapid growth of plants and weeds in the area."

While this was a decided setback to Uncle Oscar and Nurin, it was not its death knell. But other unfortunate circumstances developed, Shadyville had its quota of dim-wits, and one of them ran out of Nurin late one night. Not understanding the true nature of the fuel, he confidently supplied his tank from his own ready resources, which ruined the motor, and threw Uncle Oscar into a costly lawsuit. It seems that even dim-wits understand the use of the law.

The decisive setback came when the giant oil companies turned their backs on Nurin. It happened this way. Eager to adapt from oil to Nurin, these monster corporations competed viciously with each other in planning for the conversion. They put their brilliant idea-men on overtime searching for the advantage each needed. "Corner the urine market," was the advice of one of these brainy advisers. "How?" was the response of the executives. "Re-model all our gas stations. Put the restrooms in front. Make them so attractive and comfortable that passersby will be lured into them. Offer free oil changes or free tire-rotations as inducements," they replied. "Corner the urine market, and the formula is ours."

Draftsmen were put to work drawing plans for the new Nurin stations, and all this was done on the basis of probability, of course. Such fervor, such tension, such haste, and from all the chaos in that industry, ulcers became more prevalent than the common cold.

Back in Shadyville, Uncle Oscar chortled with glee over the great stir his invention was creating. "I'll be richer than a king," he crowed to Aunt Minnie. "Good," said Aunt Minnie. "I'll buy all the things I want starting tomorrow," and that ended his boasting right there.

The oil companies frantic plans to out-do each other ended when gas station attendants hearing of their plans refused as a body to man them, and insurance companies refused to insure them. "Selling gas is one thing," they said, "but sitting over Nurin would be like straddling an atomic bomb!"

"We refuse," said the insurance companies.

"We won't work," said the attendants.

At this point the auto manufacturers, who had taken a cautious stance, surrendered their fondest hopes and buried their soaring dreams of again turning out those luxury cars that so delighted the affluent, and enriched their makers, and returned to producing the easily crumpled miniatures with the strange names. It was a sad day in Detroit.

Here the federal government stepped in. Congress passed laws which prevented any accumulation of Nurin above a five gallon amount. This had the effect of making its sale from gas stations impossible. They also ruled that Nurin could only be used in cars in the southwestern states where lush growth would be a boon, and loud explosions would only annoy Indians.

Well, my friends, the discovery of the age went for naught. This left society on its old course toward the depletion of its energy resources, and headed for the day when the last drop of gasoline would burn up in a car going nowhere of importance, by a driver who never believed the incessant warnings that the supply was not inexhaustible. Envision that day when people will be walking around, over or through abandoned vehicles in a world without gasoline, but awash in urine and poisoned by an excess of nuclear wastes. That day you can join Uncle Oscar, who provided the solution, was rebuffed, lost a king's fortune, and weep with him in Shadyville.

########## PERPETUATION ##########

"Lies, lies, nothing but lies," muttered a disillusioned man. And, in truth, wives were lying to husbands, husbands to wives, employees to employers, employers to employees, people to the government, the government to the people, and so on, and so on--

"Why", asked the disillusioned man, "when we all start life in innocence, do we all become liars?"

"Why won't you play with me?", asked one youngster of another.

"Because you stink," answered the first as he headed home.

"Mother, I told Karl that he stinks, and I wouldn't play with him."

"You shouldn't say things like that," said his mother. "You should have said something like: "I can't play now, I've got to practice the piano."

"But you sold the piano," said the innocent one; perplexed.

"I guess you'll just have to live and learn," said the baffled mother.

One day the kid comes home from school, and no one is there. He's supposed to empty the garbage, but doesn't. His mother comes home and says sharply, "Why didn't you empty the garbage like I told you?"

"Because I had to practice the piano," answers the kid, confident that he had learned the lesson.

THE MEDDLING MOUNTAINEER   1980

With no wish to prey upon your credulity, I begin this tale with the certain expectation of generating in your minds that cloud of doubt and skepticism which is certain to surround all such tales requiring faith in the veracity of the author for belief. Being as this tale is, in reality, an account of an extravagant, even grotesque discovery, and defiant of ready acceptance because of its unusual aspects--yet necessary of relating - I proceed in the face of whatever reception its telling may have with you, my readers.

Let me first make it clear that I stumbled upon this story through my superior skill as a mountaineer; my fame in that pursuit being firmly established and beyond depreciation. As a matter of record, the Encyclopedia of Foolish Exploits, if consulted, contains sufficient proof to convince anyone of my stature in this dangerous and daring sport. Hoping now to have established my credentials to your satisfaction, let me tell my story.

Forty years ago, having bested all the mountain peaks on this continent, and in the search for new challenges elsewhere, the Casketone Range in the Far East drew my attention. Because its lofty peaks owned a deserved reputation as unconquerable among the brotherhood of mountain climbers, the desire to attempt what had so far defied all others burned so fiercely in me that came the day when I could no longer resist their lure. I saw in the defiance of the Casketones the challenge I so dearly sought, and in their conquest, the satisfaction of my thirst for fame and fortune.

Thus impelled, I arrived in Bunglersburg, the ancient and historic capital of Lurchestan, in early summer and took up residence there with the intention of making preparations for my ascent of the Casketones, which rose to dizzying heights a few miles to the south of this city. From my place of residence within Bunglersburg, I could look with awe upon their majestic slopes as they reached far into the clouds on most days; and detect their frightening ruggedness which had been sufficient to maintain a reputation as killers of all previous hopes of conquest.

From this assortment, I promptly chose Mount

Dunderhead for my adventure. This magnificent giant stood highest of all, and when visible in its entirety, showed a smoking volcanic crest which had periodically spewed out its wrath upon Bunglersburg, and all but destroyed it in the year 1648.

I spent a full month in preparing to tackle Dunderhead and it was no more time than I needed. I forwent such usual pleasures as sightseeing and picturetaking to concentrate on my main purpose for being there, success in which would establish me as the premier mountain-climber of all time. I gave even the minutest items my personal attention and being sponsored by the Society For The Perpetuation of Doubtful Endeavors did not stint where equipment and supplies were concerned. Every governmental agency of Lurchestan was put at my service, and I made good use of their generous help in soliciting not only advice, but maps, charts, accounts of previous failing attempts on Dunderhead, estimates of provisions needed, weather prognostications, geological surveys, and much more that might aid me to succeed where others had failed. I intended to succeed! I was determined to know what lay beyond their defiant summits!

Dawned the day I had chosen to begin my ascent to the very crest of the Casketones. It turned out to be not an especially auspicious one for what I proposed to do. Clouds hung low about Dunderhead Peak and portended foul weather. Nonetheless, with my purpose set in mind, I began the ascent. Hourly the difficulty increased, and at nightfall I was already behind schedule.

The anticipated storm came during the night. The howling winds and driven snow, accompanied by a sharp drop in temperature, made it a miserable experience; but this in no way exceeded previous experiences I had undergone on other occasions, and was, more or less, to be expected. The morning brought clear, cold weather, rather ideal for my purpose. I took advantage of these favorable conditions to make up for the previous day's deficiency in distance traveled upward. By nightfall of this second day I was at that point of elevation where previous climbers had begun to yield to the difficulty of further ascent. Huge snowdrifts whitened the landscape as permanent dress; the sheerness of the cliffs ahead, and the uncertain footing they offered were discouragements of considerable strength. Without having yet invaded this rocky maze, my knowledge of mountain terrain told me that yawning chasms lay between those forbidding pinnacles that rose up like giant needles along the path ahead.

After a restless night that brought nothing worse to contend with than bitter cold temperatures, which are commonly associated with such heights, I began my third day of travel upward with the trepidation that one is likely to feel before a dangerous and risky adventure. Soon I was toiling upward, progressing foot by foot, and that only after torturous effort, with risk of life and limb, through a succession of breath-taking moments. An hour of the greatest exertion, fraught with perilous possibilities, and I could have tossed a shot-put back to my former position.

By noon of that day I had come to a point where all previous attempts had ended. Before me rose a sheer rock wall of great height and steepness, without a single evidence of foot or hand-hold on its smooth face, and standing at such an angle that it leaned over me like a threatening giant. Conceding that I couldn't scale this obstacle, I moved horizontally along its base, hoping to find a more friendly contour thereby. Luck, which I readily admit to be a significant factor in mountain climbing, was with me; for I came upon a cleft in this rock wall up which I could ascend, and did. There at the top of the cliff, I found a narrow ledge running between it and the deep chasm next to be challenged. On this I rested while I eyed the possibilities now open to me for advancing on to my ultimate goal. There was some pleasure in knowing that I had already accomplished what no man before me had succeeded in doing, and stood above their best efforts. From where I sat resting, the column of acrid smoke that spiralled out of Dunderhead's yawning mouth looked encouragingly near; and a sense of triumph was already making its precocious presence felt in the pit of my stomach.

The day was wearing on, and if I were to descend down the near side of the chasm hoping to ascend the far side yet before darkness, I must be at it at once. With renewed spirits, I began making my way toward the bottom of this deep rift. Descending was not as difficult as I expected it to be, and in an hour's time I was at its foot and in almost complete darkness.

Between the two walls of this chasm was a flat, narrow ledge with good footing. Resting on this with my back against the wall I had just descended, I used my flashlight to survey the situation. Like a pathway, this ledge on which I stood ran in both directions from me. I decided to investigate, and began moving to my left along it with careful steps. Proceeding in this manner for some distance, frequently needing to wedge myself through narrow places, I saw ahead of me what appeared to be a sharp corner. I also noticed with surprise that this area was not draped in the same degree of darkness as that through which I had been winding my way. Thinking that highly unusual, and deciding to determine why, I moved to the corner and peered around it. There, most unbelievably, through a narrow defile, was daylight from the far side of the Casketones. Success was mine!

What an unexpected piece of good fortune! Success! I couldn't, for a minute, believe what I was seeing. Beyond doubt, I had discovered an unknown pass through the Casketones to lands beyond, eliminating further climbing. As I became fully aware of the significance of this discovery, disbelief taunted me. "It couldn't be--could it?" I asked myself; and then, like many another who had striven to the point of defeat and had suddenly and unexpectedly met with success, I crumpled to my haunches and shed tears of relief and ecstasy at one and the same time. I had done it! I had accomplished what no man before me had done--crossed the Casketones.

It was some time before I recovered sufficiently to press on. When able, I squeezed myself through the narrow opening between rock faces until I stood finally in the full light of day, still reeling from elation. Hastily I made camp, fearing to go further in my unsteady condition. That evening I named this gateway "The Complimentary Pass" which was mine to do by right of discovery.

The morning of my success found me rested and revitalized, and understandably eager to penetrate the ignorance and mystery surrounding the land beyond the mountains, heretofore unseen by human eyes. Dawn, that should have provided my first opportunity to survey the scene carefully, was a disappointment. Fog was everywhere and the smoke from Dunderhead's crater, which had curled upward, now took a downward course to mix with the fog and give it the stench of burning sulphur, affecting both eyes and nose disagreeably, while together obscuring effectively any hope I had of inspecting what lay below me.

I began my descent eagerly, and it was soon apparent that the northern slopes of the Casketones had little of the ruggedness of those I had just climbed. Progress downward was no problem for one of my skill. By nightfall I had descended well into the treeline, and spent the night in their comforting environment, sure that I would complete my descent on the morrow, and then know what existed below me.

When the first rays of dawn lighted up the sky next morning, I was already up and anxious. No fog, no fumes hindered my view, but the denseness of the tall forest trees, among which I had slept, did; and as I made my way downward I had to be satisfied with an occasional unsatisfying peek through their covering. From these "peeks" I concluded that I was to enter a small land area completely surrounded by towering mountains, with at least one river touring through the countryside fed by numerous creeks, and that the area was green and beautiful.

My opportunity to scout ahead was not improved when I at last reached level ground. I was still deep in the forest. Here I divested myself of my mountain-climbing paraphernalia, hiding it, for what reason I didn't know, and proceeded on at a more rapid pace with the expectant air one wears when he has no idea what he may come upon, but has great hopes none-the-less.

Before I had entirely cleared the forest, I fancied that I could smell wood smoke. "Could that be an indication of human existence," I wondered, "or, just some smouldering logs from a recent forest fire." It was not easy for me to suppose that humans could live in a land so inaccessible, so I discounted that possibility and continued on.

After what I would estimate to be about five miles, I cleared the forest; and what I saw astounded me. The area was green all right, but here and there were sod huts and stone houses from whose chimneys issued columns of smoke. Running about the countryside were fences of piled stone, evidently marking off fields, in many of which were flocks of sheep and goats. No doubt about it, this land was inhabited by humans. How human, I did not yet know, but judging from the pastoral scene before me, I held little doubt--very human.

Emboldened by this judgment, I advanced to the nearest hut. Sounds of activity inside included what I assumed to be conversation among persons. Approaching the doorway, I knocked loudly and awaited the appearance of whomever or whatever lived inside. A short silence caused by my knocking was followed by the sound of footsteps, and suddenly the door was swung open. Before me stood a tall man with a friendly look upon his face, changed instantly to one of surprise. Intending to reassure him, I hurried to explain that I was a stranger, had just crossed the mountains (pointing to them as added assistance to his understanding), and would appreciate some information. I spoke without thinking that I might not be understood. The man stood eyeing me with suspicion that grew as I talked. Thinking that he couldn't understand me, I repeated what I had said in a louder voice, and looked to him for some evidence of comprehension.

Soon he broke out into a broad smile, pushed the door open wider, and in words I could understand invited me to enter. I walked past him into the room somewhat apprehensively, not knowing what to expect there. The room was small and dark. Before me was a large table, at the far end of which sat a woman, and along its length two children, a boy of perhaps eight or ten and a girl somewhat younger. I paused just inside the door, undecided about my next move. When the man motioned me toward a seat at the opposite end of the table from the woman, I proceeded to seat myself there. He then closed the door and proceeded to seat himself beside his children and near to his wife. As he moved, I was immediately conscious that his one leg was a good foot shorter than the other, causing him to walk with a pronounced hitching motion. Believing him to be crippled, I made as if I didn't notice his impairment, and nodding in friendly fashion to the woman and the two children waited for what was to come.

For a short time no one spoke. I was conscious that I was being closely inspected by all and beginning to feel self-conscious about it, which induced me to interrupt the silence to repeat that I was a stranger, had just crossed the mountains, and desired information.

The man looked at his wife for a moment after I spoke, then turning towards me, burst out laughing. Soon all four were laughing loudly as if I had said something that struck them as exceedingly humorous. Not knowing what to make of this behavior, I wore a look of amazement on my face. After turning back to face me, the man ceased laughing and the others followed suit. Sensing my discomfort, the man remarked: "You must be mistaken, sir, there is no other side of these mountains. We were just enjoying your joke."

That he spoke in Salwanese, which I too both spoke and understood, was a great relief to me. I was delighted that we could converse, but his assertion confounded me.

"Why", I asked, "do you say that there is no other side of the mountains? I don't understand what you mean. All mountains have two sides," I added.

"Oh, no!" he replied. "No! There is nothing beyond the mountains but empty space. Absurdia is all there is."

"Absurdia? What is Absurdia?", I asked.

"This is Absurdia", he answered, pointing to the floor.

"Absurdia is the name of this country?" I asked, hoping I had understood him correctly.

"Yes, this is the Kingdom of Absurdia. There is nothing else."

So positive was he that I thought better of trying to convince him otherwise, and was about to change the subject when the woman, apologizing for her lack of hospitality, rose to correct that omission. To my continued surprise she too was crippled, and in the same manner as her husband, having one leg much shorter than the other.

It was then that the children, having finished their breakfast, left the room for some activity out-of-doors. When I saw that they too bore the same affliction I was hard put to refrain from inquiring the cause; but not wishing to violate their hospitality, I held back.

Having been seated this length of time in the gloomy interior of the hut, my eyes grew adjusted to the dim light, and details of its construction became visible. Besides containing the rude table and benches, the room had a fireplace for warmth. Cooking pots of cast iron and crockery of baked clay were arrayed on a shelf near the fireplace. At the far end of the room was a curtained doorway which must have led to sleeping quarters. It was a rustic and simple dwelling. That they suffered many inconveniences was undeniable from the evidence.

To continue the conversation in a different vein, I asked the man if he would explain to me the geography of Absurdia, as I intended to find out all I could about it. Most obligingly he did so, and with an amount of pride in the telling that could only come from one who loved his homeland.

Absurdia's kingdom, it seemed, was small in area--perhaps 500 square miles--oval in shape, surrounded on all sides by mountains. The geographic center of the country was the site of the only city in the kingdom, called Outlandish. The King and Queen resided there in their palace, he said, King Hefty and his beloved Queen Heftier, as he informed me they were named, were spoken of with so much love and affection that it was obvious to me immediately I was in a happy land and among contented people.

Wishing to begin my tour of the kingdom without delay, I expressed my appreciation for kindnesses received and took my departure from the Stumbles--for so they were named. Because they had so admired my wrist watch, I made them a gift of it on parting.

I set my course for Outlandish along a well-defined road. Before long, I saw approaching me from the opposite direction a party of four Absurdians, all on foot, of course. Not yet entirely certain of my reception in this land, being a stranger, I stood watching them come. At once I could see that here were four more crippled individuals; their method of progress left no doubt of it. Almost in unison they dipped to one side, then straightened, then dipped, then straightened; and strangely enough, moved forward toward me very slowly. Their paths of travel were a series of circles, each one a short distance in front of the last. This I could see was due to their impairment. The circumstance was that their short leg advanced very little as they walked along, serving more as a pivot than as a means of forward movement. The normal leg being moved forward a respectable distance caused them to progress in a series of circles that, if diagrammed, would give the same appearance as a stretched coil spring.

Finally they drew close to me. My curiosity was now of such proportion that I could no longer resist the desire to know why so many--in fact all--Absurdians were deformed. So I accosted one of them.

"I am a stranger here," I said, "Would you be so kind as to tell me what caused you to be crippled?"

"Crippled?" he replied in a tone that indicated resentment. "I am not crippled! Why do you ask such a question?"

"But your legs--"

"What's wrong with my legs?" he asked peevishly.

"Why, one is so much shorter than the other," I answered, pointing at the short one.

"How else?" he replied; then noticing that I was differently constructed he added, "There is nothing unusual about that! Now you are crippled in my opinion. How do you explain your two legs of the same length?"

I didn't know how to reply, I was set back by this seeming contradiction of what to me was normality in the human anatomy. When they passed on, laughing to themselves, I was relieved, and I looked down at my two good legs with a new regard, "Crippled!" I said to myself. Never had I thought to be so designated, "How odd it is when a normal man is regarded as crippled, and a crippled man declares himself normal. My mind whirled in confusion.

I continued on my way, meeting other Absurdians at intervals, all of whom were crippled and walked in circles; and many of whom turned, after I passed by to look at me quizzically, as if asking themselves how one could be born with two equal legs. Others showing concern for my "crippled" condition with a look of sympathy playing over their faces.

Filled with curiosity, I proceeded on. Coming in time to the city of Outlandish, which was not the vast metropolis I expected, but rather that sort of population center we might call a good-sized village. From my first glimpse of it, I decided it to be appropriately named. All buildings of any size--and there weren't too many fitting that category--were round in shape, and the people's homes all seemed to be in clusters inside circular streets, much like grill-work in effect. At the heart of the city stood the only imposing building visible; the palace of King Hefty and Queen Heftier, I had no doubt. The city was laid out as it was, I ventured to guess, to best accommodate the walking patterns of Absurdians with their one short leg.

The palace was my destination, and I was too tired to wish to walk in circles to get there; so I took a cross-lots path directly at it. If Absurdians indulge in profanity, that must be what several householders aimed my way as I leaped their fences and trod through their yards. My formal education in Salwanese, I know, didn't include any of the words or expressions shouted--even screamed--at me along the way.

My course being accurate, I arrived at the palace, a white marble edifice, round, of course, two stories high, very ornamental, with carved figures at intervals, and with carved lettering over its main entrance announcing that all were free to enter. I accepted that invitation and passing through its portals found myself in a circular hallway that appeared to run completely around the building, and off which were numerous doorways to the interior. Each door bore a sign announcing the name of a person and his title, much as it is in our own state capitols.

I made the complete circuit, reading each sign as I passed it. Tax collector Surveyor, Judge, I passed them all including the Health Officer's office, which I had a sudden urge to avoid lest I be detained because of my "crippled" condition. Part way around the circular hallway I came to two huge oaken doors bearing metal signs: "King Hefty" on one, "Queen Heftier" on the other, and underneath each the word "Enter". Accepting this as an invitation to anyone, including strange "cripples", I did so.

The door opened on a suite of rooms. I was not far inside when I heard a pleasant female voice say, "My dear, we must do more for the Uplanders." This was followed by a masculine voice in answer saying, "You are right as always dearest." Moving in the direction of the voices, I entered an interior room where I spied the Queen sitting in a large chair knitting something that looked like a rug. Across from her, sprawled in another chair was King Hefty. One brief espial and I acknowledged to myself that their names were most appropriate. Both were extremely fat with round, rosy, bulging cheeks and several chins apiece. They hadn't yet noticed my presence when I spoke:

"Your Majesties," I said, bowing, "May I come in?"

Slightly startled by my intrusion, the Queen rose with extraordinary difficulty as if to see me the better, and the King remaining seated turned my way quickly and said in a cheerful tone of voice: "Certainly, all may enter here. You must know that."

Well, I didn't; but I was pleased to hear him say so. I approached King Hefty's chair, bowed again, and was about to speak when the Queen, to whom I now had my back turned, in a tone of great pity said:

"The poor man is deformed. Oh, my! How can we help you?"

There it was again, this contradiction of circumstance; for it was they, not I, who had the shortened leg. What good would it do me to protest. At least, I thought, here I am receiving sympathetic regard, not the ridicule shown me along the way.

"Your Majesty," I said, addressing the King once more, "I am here as a foreigner in your beautiful kingdom, I only came upon it by chance after crossing the Casketone Mountains. People on my side of the mountains are unaware that the Kingdom of Absurdia exists. While I am here it is my wish to learn all I can about you, your people, and your kingdom. Your Majesty, I beg your permission to do this. Will you please grant my request?"

Before I had completed my petition to the King, I was conscious that Queen Heftier, facing me at all times, had sidled toward King Hefty's chair. By the time I had finished she stood leaning against him, timorously regarding me and looking at the king with eyes that expressed apprehension and incredulity.

There was silence for a time during which the two whispered back and forth. Finally, the King leaned forward in his chair, and the Queen drifted behind him as if shielding herself from danger. The King spoke:

"Sir, I don't know who you pretend to be. You say you are a stranger from the other side of the mountains. That is a peculiar statement for a sane man to make. There is no other side of the mountains as you should know: Absurdia is all there is! To say otherwise is to cast doubt on your sanity! I do not like this!" he concluded.

"But your Majesty!----". I started to protest. This ignorance of true geography appalled me, then I recalled how I had heard this same statement from the Stumbles and from the man on the road. Without question this was general belief among all Absurdians, and the "why" of it intrigued me.

As I hesitated to continue, and seemed speechless for the moment, King Hefty arose from his chair, pulled himself up to his regal best attitude, and addressed me so:

"Young man," he said, "you appear here walking on two legs of equal length, suggesting that you are from the other side of the mountains; and by saying so, inferring that Absurdia is not all there is. At first I was inclined to regard you with sympathy because of your obvious deformity, but your statements in our royal presence are intolerable. Under our laws you are guilty of blasphemous utterances, and I cannot nor will not let your crime go unpunished. I declare you to be demented, a madman, and I intend to have you confined at once."

There was something commanding in his manner and tone of voice, and in the firmness of his decision. I thought to run, but before I could move, both the King and Queen walked past me and in great haste fled the room, shouting for help. Assistance came quickly from all directions as uniformed men, palace guards I assumed, grabbed me roughly, immobilized my arms and legs, picked me up bodily and carried me off. Never having considered such a possibility, knowing that I was free of any bad intention, the thought of being imprisoned as a madman offered a subduing prospect. "Absurdia is all there is," I told myself as I was being transported away, "and you'd better believe it," I admonished myself. Of course, I couldn't accept this evaluation any more than I could agree that the moon was made of green cheese; but I had no wish to become a martyr to a false belief. "But, until I get out of Absurdia, that's going to be the way it is," I said aloud. "Who can convince the blissfully ignorant!" I asked myself. "And what would be the good in trying."

I was carried some distance down the circular hallway to a small room where I was deposited roughly on a wall bench, the only article of furniture in the entire room. My porters, having fulfilled their orders, left immediately, leaving me alone and unattended. I heard them lock the door as they left. I was a prisoner by circumstance.

The tour down the hallway had been made with the assistance of six men, three on each side of me. Those on my left had short left legs; those on my right had short right legs. As they conveyed me to my place of detention, I found myself being tilted now to the left and again to the right as first one row of my bearers dipped on their short legs in unison at the same time as the other row rose on their long legs. What resulted was a wave-like action down a zigzag course. Clever arrangement I thought, and representing the only example of cooperation between persons so deformed I could think of. I supposed that King Hefty had employed these guards with that in mind.

I looked over my place of incarceration carefully. It seemed far from impregnable. As a matter of fact, the two windows it contained could be easily pried open, and when I tried the door at the rear of the room, it was unlocked, "These people," I opined, "were either of a trusting nature, or too simple-minded for their own good."

I walked out of my place of detention directly into the hallway that encircled the palace. A few Absurdians were hitching their way along its route, They paid no attention to me at first; then one, who must have noticed my level walk, showed an intention of making it a point of sympathetic comment. I hurried past her, and with a prudence that seems to me now indicative of good sense, I began to pretend a hitch in my walk, which sufficed to withdraw me from further notice.

I hitched my way out of the city of Outlandish to the farmlands surrounding it. By this time I had a hip so sore from improper use that I could no longer navigate in the Absurdian manner. I sat down upon a rock fence to rub the hip, rest and gather my wits. "Should I flee back to Lurchestan, or stay and gather data on this weird culture." I debated this for some time as I stretched my aching leg and rubbed my sore hip back to fully operational condition.

Discretion argued for flight; curiosity egged me on to remain. These two impulses fenced with each other in my thoughts until curiosity won out. I couldn't leave Absurdia without learning more about it.

The decision made; thus prompted, my next move demanded thought. Knowing now that Absurdians were gullible, that their general mentality was that of children, that they showed an unusual good-heartedness; and feeling certain that as long as I didn't challenge their erroneous belief that 'Absurdia is all there is', I could move about freely, I turned back toward Outlandish, there to pursue my quest for information.

After my unhappy experience at the palace, I chose to be wary of again going near it. Instead, I headed along a street that circled the outskirts of the city with the intention of visiting areas I had not yet been in. On my way I spared myself what grief I could by walking with a hitch only when being observed. Here, on the east side of Outlandish, something struck me as different, but I couldn't at first decide, what it was. My puzzlement was over when it came to me that the citizens on the east side of town were circling counterclockwise in their walk; where as those on the west side had circled clockwise. This I quickly realized was due to a shortness of the left leg on the east siders and of the right leg of the west siders. What significance was contained in this observation I did not yet know.

I seated myself on a park bench along side one of the circular streets to rest my sore leg, just as a passerby wound his way toward me. He approached as if desiring to offer conversation. He had no suspicion of me, so I welcomed him. He took his seat beside me following a brief exchange of greetings, seemed to be in a leisurely mood, and gave indication of being quite talkative. He was an elderly person, bearded and wrinkled. He, it was, who initiated our conversation.

"I need to rest once and a while", he said as he adjusted himself in his seat. "The name is Tilted", he added.

"That I can understand," I replied as I curled one leg beneath. the bench so he would not notice my "crippled" condition. "Pleased to make your acquaintance," I added.

"We Uplanders," he continued, have some nice places to sit and rest. The Downlanders do not. And your name, sir?" Caught by surprise I came up with "Hitcher" which I hoped would satisfy him then ventured to say: "I take it you are an

"Uplander," not realizing how close I was to making another serious mistake.

"Who else!" he answered as if surprised by the stupidity of my inquiry. "No Downlander had better show up here."

"Yes, of course," I replied, "We don't want them here, do we?"

"They never cross the line between us. They know better than that," he stated with conviction. "My grandfather," he went on, "tells me how confused life was when we did live together. All that bumping into one another."

"It's best to be separated," I offered.

"Oh, yes!" said he, "King Hefty got things straightened out when he ordered that all Uplanders must live on the east side of Outlandish, and all Downlanders on the west side. Wise man, King Hefty," he added as if thoroughly convinced of it.

"You seem to know a good deal about our history," I said, "being much younger than you, I don't have your advantage". (By using the pronoun "our" I was hoping to disguise my true identity much the same way as I did when I curled my leg under the bench.)

"Few Absurdians know about our history because only a handful can read, or want to read. I am one of that few", he stated proudly.

"I am one of the many," I lied. "I can't read."

"Too bad," he said sympathetically. "Through reading I am aware of facts about our land that I dare not admit to knowing." This he offered in lowered tones as if confiding in me.

"Oh!" I said, suddenly interested. "If I could read I wouldn't know where to get information." With this I hoped to glean from him the location of the reading materials he had consulted,

"Few know that," he answered, then added: "I was one of King Hefty's Counsellors for many years. This provided me with access to the documents in his library, so I read them secretly when the king and queen were away, The complete history of Absurdia is there, you know. If I had been caught I wouldn't be here now."

"Is that right!", I said, as if surprised to hear it--which I was. "In the library," I added to emphasize the point. "But aren't you still in grave danger?" I asked.

"Well," he said, rising quickly as if to avoid further conversation. "I must get on. Absurdia is all there is. Nice to meet you," and he was on his way abruptly.

I was preoccupied with my thoughts for a while. How could I get into King Hefty's library, I wondered. There I could learn all I needed to know about Absurdians, if I could manage that. My earlier experience at the palace, with its wide openness to the public, made the possibility seem well within the scope of my talents as an enterprising individual. I decided on the attempt. Accordingly I hitched my way to the palace, and without drawing any unusual attention to myself approached the doors to King Hefty's domain. As before, they opened readily. I listened carefully for a moment, then slipped in and closed the doors. Quickly I slid behind some draperies nearby, and again listened attentively for any sound of occupancy. In a short while I heard footsteps coming down the circular stairway that led to rooms above. Peeking out from behind the draperies, I saw that it was Queen Heftier in all her obese magnificence. Once at the bottom of the staircase she paused with one hand on the newel, puffing hard from the exertion. When composed she called lustily upward:

"Are you coming?" she shouted, as if annoyed by some delay.

"Immediately, dear," was the obedient response from the upper regions. I recognized King Hefty's voice, and watched him hobble his way down.

"Now remember," spoke the queen, "if you are to please the Uplanders you must concede them something. And you must do that in such a way as will not stir up animosity with the Downlanders. Do you understand?" she asked sternly and in that tone of voice a wife uses to firmly implant an idea in a husband's simple mind.

"Yes, dear," was his weak response. "Shall we go?", and they both walked by my hiding place on their way out.

After the door closed, and the sound of their footsteps melted away, I emerged from behind the drapes, secure in the belief that I was alone in the room before I began my search for the King's library. It was not here, it was not there. As it turned out I did locate it in the cellar below, then spent some moments deciding my next move. I was engaged in a risky venture, and knew I would be a fool to examine the documents where I found them. Besides, the atmosphere was too dingy and dark for easy reading; so I gathered them in my arms--they were parchment rolls--one armful accommodating the entire collection, and headed for the room in which I had earlier been held a prisoner. Making sure that I would not be seen, I ran down the hall and entered by the same door through which I had escaped and with the same ease as I had fled from it. Here I had little fear of interruption, I felt secure in the belief that any chance of being interrupted was negligible.

The reading of the hand-written manuscripts was difficult, but most enlightening. By the time I had waded through them all, I knew what I wanted to know--the whys and wherefores that accounted for the hidden Kingdom of Absurdia--and it was an astounding account, I assure you.

To begin with, back many hundreds of years ago, this landlocked piece of real estate, it seemed, had been accidentally discovered by a group of persons out of Bunglersburg in Lurchestan; who, being pursued by the then King of Lurchestan, one Smasher II, a beast in king's robes, whose appetite for cruelty had driven many to seek escape, and whose repressive policies had been responsible for innumerable deaths among his subjects, as well as inestimable torture and suffering for others. Knowing that capture meant certain death, with nothing to lose, these desperate people fleeing in terror braved the rigors of the Casketones, and with the loss of several lives enroute, succeeded in crossing them to become the true discoverers of this hidden land.

This knowledge chastened me. That I was not the first to cross the Casketones created in me a strong resentment toward those who had cheated me of the glory I was exulting in. For a moment I considered hiding the actual story on my return, and claiming the credit myself--but couldn't in actuality.

From these few survivors all Absurdians descended. They kept their native language, of course and this erased my wonder at hearing Salwanese spoken in so isolated a spot. Although the population grew steadily, it was many long years before the inhabitants chose to organize a government. When they did, there was no dispute on its character. The only major concern was who should be the first king.

Now King Hefty's direct ancestor, far removed, was the strongest candidate for that position, mostly because he looked like a king should look, commanded like a king should command, and had the most voters under obligation. But the truth was that for all his imposing appearance and regal bearing, he was somewhat of a fake, more of a pretender, and a complete example of the efficacy of shrewdness over wisdom. He was accordingly the people's choice and was crowned King Knotalther, to begin his reign over Absurdia.

King Knotalther may have lacked wisdom, but not courage. Under his rule the country grew and prospered, and admiration for him grew likewise. At the height of his popularity, King Knotalther, intending to act in the best interest of his subjects, called all adults of the new kingdom to a conference. No adult, well or ill, young or old dared pass up this conference under the threat of death; so all appeared, walking, riding, or borne on a litter. No child under twelve was permitted to attend, unless too young to comprehend what would take place at the conference.

Once the crowd was assembled in a large field, King Knotalther addressed them, presenting his plan for the eternal preservation of Absurdia. "Beginning this instant," he announced, "no child of ours shall ever be told that the world is comprised of anything more than Absurdia. They shall remain forever ignorant of the evil world outside. They shall be taught that the crests of these mountains that surround us (here he made a broad sweep with his arms) measures the limits of the world. Bring them up with this statement on their lips," he commanded, "'Absurdia is all there is!' There will be no exceptions! Do not defy my orders on pain of death!"

From that day to this it was so. The new generation arose totally convinced that it was so; and as the years passed and those who knew better died, it became so.

Here I suddenly recalled the statement of Tilted when he confided in me that he possessed knowledge that could endanger his life if known. He obviously knew that Absurdia was not all the world contained. This was dangerous knowledge in Absurdia, I now realized, and explained his abrupt departure when I, unknowingly, neared the subject.

King Knotalther's idea had its merits, you must admit. Living in the security of complete isolation, Absurdians could, and did, until I crossed the Casketones, live with no concern for anything other than their own welfare, and in peace and harmony. King Knotalther was hailed the genius he appeared to be. Then the good folk of Absurdia prepared to depart.

But the children! What happened to the children during their absence from their parents supervision? I'm afraid they did not fare well. Separating them in congregation was an unwise act by King Knotalther. "They will all be taken to Yelping Valley," he had ordered, "where they can amuse themselves until their parents return for them." From the viewpoint of amusement the King picked an ideal spot. Yelping Valley had an abundance of intriguing diversions for young children. There were stones for throwing, sharp sticks for sticking, pools of water for splashing, mud holes for daubing, a river for drowning, and hay stacks for smothering. What more could youngsters want? In no time they were making full use of these play things so generously supplied by kind Mother Nature. The number of black eyes, bumps, scratches, cuts, lost teeth, and the amount of skin and hair removed from faces, arms and heads may have established some kind of record in length of time for accomplishment.

With these inspired activities at their peak and cries of pain and shouts of glee competing equally for volume in decibels of sound, suddenly the children became conscious of an alien presence. Coming as if from nowhere was a wrinkled, dirty, ugly, dishevelled, evil-looking old hag who stood staring upon them with dark intent. Those nearest her shrank back, and some began to cry and cower in fear; others stood frozen and white-faced unable to move. Slowly the old hag began to circle the group, snarling and uttering threats. Terror showed in many eyes and on drawn faces; partly, at least, from recognition of who she was and of what evil-powers were known to be consigned to her. Yes! Her reputation for evil doing was well known to the children from often-told tales warning them against just this kind of contact with her. "Beware of Gotcha, the Witch of the Mountain" had been a constant admonition; and the phrase "Gotcha'll gitcha, if you don't behave" was now echoing through their consciousness.

All to no avail! The genius of King Knotalther was here, at this moment, under a shadow of gravest doubt and suspicion.

Round and round them the Witch wound her way, slowly compacting the children into a crowded, shuddering, bawling, intense mass of almost hysterical juveniles. Once satisfied in her intent, Gotcha uttered a shrieking command: "Quiet, I say!" and dead silence, excepting for an uncontrollable whimper here and there, reigned among them. Eyes displaying terror-stricken thoughts stared at the witch who cackled with satisfaction over the effect she had created among them.

"Hear me now!" she screeched in her shrill voice, "listen closely, my dears, and mind what I say! Lies and falsehoods have been told you about me. They are not so! You shall know my true story." This was said with a waving of bony arms for emphasis. She continued: "I was once a s-w-e-e-t child like you--or you--or you." Gotcha pointed a sharp finger at selected small girls as she said this, causing those indicated to cringe even more and hide their faces in their hands.

Proceeding, the witch added: "King Knotalther--curses be on his foul head - banished me forever, he did, from Absurdia to a cave in the mountains all without reason or cause. It was there that I swore vengeance on him and all his miserable subjects. Many years have I waited! Many years have I suffered! Many years have I nursed my hatred! I was not idle though. Oh, no! was not idle!" Here she produced the nearest thing in her repertoire resembling a smile of satisfaction, which only served to screw her ugly face into a more repulsive expression. "I studied to learn the ways of the Sisterhood of Black Powers," she resumed, "and became one of their select society. Why--you wish to know why?" No one had inquired of anything, of course, "Why else, but to prepare me for this very moment. How delighted I am," she screamed, "that King Knotalther's stupidity has become my long awaited chance for revenge." Here she laughed so hard and with such uncontrollable glee that she fell into a fit, rolling over and over on the ground, doubled up from the pain of it. Finally she regained her poise, rose from the ground and stood with arms upraised as if appealing to invisible beings. "Now, Oh Spirits of the Nether World, favor me that I may avenge myself for the many wrongs done me. Grant me the power to avenge myself in full measure,

I beg of you, Oh Spirits of the Depths."

After this demonstration, the infamous Gotcha, the Witch of the Mountain, began chanting and dancing about in a small circle. As she continued in this act, louder and louder grew her incantations until they rose to a shrieking crescendo. The frightened children watched spellbound and immobilized. After a period of dancing and imploring invisible spirits she suddenly stopped, stood for a moment in awful silence as if listening for a reply to her request; then uttering an ear-piercing screech, jumped high in the air with arms thrashing and fell in a heap upon the ground. There to remain inert for several tense moments. Arising then, slowly, with the most evil leer upon her ugly face, she addressed her startled audience thus: "My wish has now been granted! The power to avenge myself is mine! You, (here she pointed directly at the huddled children), you must pay for the wrongs of your foul king and your hated parents--and how you'll pay, my dears!" she added. This time she croaked and cackled in the most unearthly manner. It was obvious that she was exceedingly pleased with herself and meant to enjoy her revenge to the utmost.

Bending over, she picked from the ground a stick which she held with one end in each hand. She raised her arms above her head while uttering some strange imprecation. Instantly, for no apparent reason, the stick, of itself, snapped right in two. Holding the two halves out for inspection, she threw both at the circle of children, shouting exultingly: "It is done! Revenge is mine" and slowly walked away in the direction of her mountain cave, cackling in deep satisfaction.

The children never moved or uttered a sound until she was out of sight. Then in panic, they fled in all directions on trembling legs, to be located later by their concerned parents after long search, cowering under bushes, in ditches, hidden in hay stacks, sheds, anywhere they could hide themselves.

Now King Knotalther, as a result of this fiasco, was royally berated and would certainly have been dethroned--if not beaten to death--had Gotcha's curse produced an immediate noticeable result. But the children, when calmed down and reassured, resumed their normal lives, evidently unchanged. This puzzled the good citizens of Absurdia; yet, at the same time, relieved their uneasy minds. So King Knotalther survived, but a stigma was on his reputation from that time on.

Normal living resumed in Absurdia and fears dwindled to nothing. Some Absurdians even developed doubts that the Witch Gotcha possessed any real evil powers, and a few, who were tenderhearted to a fault, even petitioned the King for a revocation of her banishment--unsuccessfully.

Some years later it was that the older girls among those present on that awful day came of childbearing age. At first it was regarded as a mere birth defect that their offspring entered the world with a pronounced deformity-one leg of each was shorter than the other by the same length as either half of the stick that had snapped in two so mysteriously in the hands of Gotcha. This then was her curse, delayed in its sorry effect. Realization came swiftly and suddenly. All children born of those mothers stained by the curse suffered that same handicap. As you can guess, with time, all children born in Absurdia were likewise crippled, and when I arrived there a century or two later, this being the universal condition, it had long since been accepted as the normal state of being. Because no one knew otherwise, or felt more impaired than his neighbor, all regarded themselves as normal persons (which causes me to reflect that it is the differences among persons, not the similarities, that breed problems in human society).

Thus I unravelled the strange story of the Kingdom of Absurdia. "What a tale," I said to myself, "and how can I expect belief if I relate it back home." Without an answer to my question, I began consideration of just how I would go about returning the manuscripts to their place of hiding. Why they were hidden from general knowledge I now knew, and I wondered too if King Hefty or Queen Heftier knew.

I gathered up the manuscripts in my arms, opened the door of the "lock-up" a crack, and surveyed the hallway. There was activity at the moment. I waited patiently, and after a brief period the foot-traffic cleared. Taking a chance, I dashed into the hallway and ran as fast as I could go to the door of the King's quarters, barged in, and quickly shut the doors behind me, not knowing if I had been observed or not. Once inside I laid the manuscripts on a convenient table and began a stealthy inspection of my pathway back to the cellar. All seemed clear, so I returned, collected the manuscripts in my arms and tiptoed through the rooms between and down the stairs to the King's library. Each manuscript had its cubbyhole, and it took a few moments to restore them to their assigned places. How it was that I came up one short I couldn't understand. I checked them over again with the same result. Had I dropped one in the hallway as I sped along, or had I dropped one inside the King's suite? Unless I came upon it on my way out I decided I hadn't the time or opportunity to search for it. As it was, I had put my life in more jeopardy than I wished. I was considerably troubled by the consequences of my carelessness, but never did locate the missing item, I regret to say.

I used all my former strategies in leaving the palace and, hitching along most convincingly, made my way to safety. Along the way I once again came to that wayside park where I had earlier encountered Tilted, the retired King's Counsellor. I decided to rest a moment on my way out of Outlandish, and while seated there contemplating my faux pas, I recalled that Tilted knew what the manuscripts contained and must therefore be fully aware that Absurdia was not all there was.

After deliberating I decided I would be safe in confiding my true identity to him and in confessing to him that I had misplaced one of the manuscripts. It was a long shot, but if he knew what I knew, and I was sure he did, he was in the same danger as I. Besides I was becoming more and more fearful that, by my unpardonable act, I might well have set the stage for the undoing of King Knotalther's great stroke of wisdom. That I had to do something seemed imperative.

I supposed my chances of meeting Tilted to be remote in prospect, but he was a gregarious person I thought. To make myself the more conspicuous, I walked up and down--or should I say, around--the circular roadway on the chance he might be where he could catch a glimpse of me. Having no luck, I returned to the park bench and waited. An hour passed, and numerous pedestrians hobbled by--but not Tilted. I was about ready to concede to disappointment when I looked up, and there he came. I hailed him as he approached and beckoned him to a seat beside me.

"Bless my soul!" he said good-naturedly, "I never expected to see you again."

"Under normal circumstances you wouldn't have," I

replied, "but as I am caught up in unusual circumstances and need your help badly, I sought you out."

"Oh!" he said. "I don't believe your circumstances were normal last time we met, were they?"

"You are right!" I responded. "I doubted then that I had fooled you!"

"Well, to tell you the truth," he replied, "you aroused my suspicion. Something about you--the name you gave yourself, for example--gave me the impression that you were not what you seemed to be. The Hitchers are not of your build".

"I'm ashamed," I said, "Forgive my deceit. I've come here to meet you again," I added, "because I am sure you are the only person in whom I dare confide, and I must talk to someone."

"I'm flattered," he said, "If you regard me as trustworthy, use me. What's your problem?" he asked.

I was still a little hesitant to reveal my true identity and recite my tale to one whom I knew so little about; but as I looked into his eyes, I saw that he advertised his trustworthiness from those portals as well. So I began by introducing myself, admitting the facts about my presence in Absurdia, watching his expression as I did so. He was not overwhelmed at what I told him. This encouraged me to admit the loss of the manuscript. This really upset him, and he rose and paced back and forth for a while like one overwrought and imagining a calamity about to happen. Finally he returned to his seat beside me and said;

"Do you realize the consequences that could befall Absurdia if that lost manuscript happens to be found by someone who can read? Why, the whole myth that 'Absurdia is all there is,' would be shattered in an instant and consternation would result. It could be the cause of civil strife," he asserted forcefully.

"I most certainly do!" I answered, "That is exactly why I have come to you at risk of my life."

"Yes! Yes! I see that now," he said sympathetically, calming himself somewhat, "I must take care of the matter myself. It is too risky for you. Take my advice," he said, "and high-tail it out of Absurdia, back to your own people, where you will be safe. I know how violent we Absurdians can become when our fair land, or its security are at stake. Take my advice and leave at once!" He was pleading with me, and his earnest manner made compliance seem imperative.

I hated to throw the burden of my carelessness upon his shoulders, but my mission was completed; so I thanked him sincerely, shook his hand, and bade him goodbye. "I shall always remain grateful to you and regard you with friendship," were my parting words to him. So I left Absurdia to recross the Casketones.

At this present moment I am seated at my writing desk, having just completed this account of my adventure in the Kingdom of Absurdia. So many years have flown by that my memory has been taxed to recall certain details; but I assure you that this tale is accurate in essence.

From my room I turn in my chair to gaze upon the array of distant peaks that are the Casketone Mountains. Yes! I returned to Bunglersburg, believing that in this atmosphere I could best summon up those recollections necessary to my story and revive those feelings and sensations that were so much a part of it. In this I was correct! I have needed but to view the column of smoke from Dunderhead's snowy crest, measure by eye the perilous route I took up its slopes, or once again in imagination squeeze my way through the Complimentary Pass to bring back to memory so much that I had forgotten, and that with its old vividness and clarity.

Why, you wonder, have I waited until this late date to reveal what I have known all these years? For two important reasons. First: I have long been tormented by the fear that by exposing this private knowledge I could endanger the safety and security of the Kingdom of Absurdia. Recently, however, I have reassessed that prospect, and concluded that not one of you-- my dear readers--will believe a word of it. On the contrary, you are certain to regard it as this author's fanciful creation and nothing more. Thus, that fear is erased. Secondly: I have been, and still am, the victim of a guilty conscience, and because of it have suffered all the agony of mind and soul that guilt generates in a caring heart. Being again in Bunglersburg, and gazing on the Casketones has only heightened the uneasiness that gnaws at me; and I catch myself scanning their crests for any indication of a party of disillusioned Absurdians descending there, who, through my dereliction in losing a manuscript, may have discovered what King Knotalther, with benevolent intent, kept from them. In a thousand dreams they have done just that, and descending those slopes have shouted "Absurdia is not all there is!" So am I haunted even in my sleep.

Then, too, thoughts of that wonderful, elderly gentleman, Tilted, increases my remorse. The uncertainty of his fate aggravates my guilty conscience still further. That I left him to shoulder my problems and may thereby have exposed him to grave danger--perhaps even death--floods my being with shame and disgrace. That I have suffered greatly from loss of peace of mind and have paid a dear price in regret would be all too apparent to you, dear readers, could you see me now, in my present state of premature old age, broken in health. How my hand trembles as I write these words.

But your sympathy is not what I seek! How I would like to recoup lost respect in your eyes--and in my own. All I can offer to accommodate this vain hope, I'm afraid, is to inform you that until now I have never once revealed one word about the existence of the Kingdom of Absurdia; nor have I sought to claim the honor and glory that was rightfully mine by reason of discovery and conquest. This I have done to protect the people of Absurdia, whose right to live contentedly in their hidden land under a fallacious belief I deeply respect and wholeheartedly approve.

To the end of my days my fondest hope will be that, in the land of Absurdia, the Uplanders and Downlanders both will forever continue to believe that "Absurdia Is All There Is!"

######### OBSERVATION #########

Leaves are falling, hunters are afield, temperatures are falling, corn is yielding to the reapers, silos are being filled, and orchards are groaning as aching branches hold up a bountiful crop. The countryside is beautiful with radiant colors of tree leaves, the dun-colored shades of ripened crops, and the patterned faces of newly planted fields. All this so pleasant to the eye, and all this scented heavily with perfume of freshly spread manure. It is fall.

FEMALE INGENUITY   1981

Angus and Bessie McDuff had been man and wife these past 30 years. Theirs was a happy union in which Angus, like most mistaken men considered himself dominant. Bessie, who humored him in this false belief knew that she, not he, made the decisions. Bessie could correctly say that she understood Angus completely, could see right through him, could read him like an open book. Angus, on the other hand, would admit privately that he never thoroughly understood Bessie, and, for that matter, women in general. "Sometimes they don't make any sense," he opined. Still, Angus had a strong affection for his Bessie; and Bessie, the more out-going of the two was never reluctant to admit that she "loved the old coot," as she endearingly called Angus. Their marriage was founded on granite.

On one certain morning, Angus, a farmer, arose from bed cross and out-of-sorts because the weather did not favor his plans for the day. At the breakfast table he allowed his sour disposition to show by criticizing the toast, predicting disaster for the country, and castigating the minister of their church. On leaving the house for the day's work, in the autumn's darkness of early morning, he tripped over a flower pot that Bessie had carelessly left on the back stoop, fell heavily to the ground skinning his elbow and shoving his nose in the dirt. This, of course, added considerably to his ill-humor. The sounds that came to Bessie's tender ears through the thickness of the closed door, though undecipherable, nevertheless bore the unmistakable flavor of vile expression, and alerted Bessie to what might be in store for her should Angus' day not improve drastically.

Bessie had run to the window to nervously observe the results of Angus' fall. She watched as he got to his feet, kicked the broken pieces of flower pot to Kingdom Come, and stalked off in irate fashion for the barn. Here Bessie offers up a little prayer that the rest of his day would be serene and soothe his wrought up passions.

Unfortunately, the prayer went for naught. Angus' day got worse by the hour. The pitchfork handle snapped in two just as he was lofting some straw for bedding, showering him with needle-like bits and pieces that found their way inside his shirt, there to prickle and itch to his continued exasperation. It was not much later when Flossie, his favorite milch cow, stepped on his foot, causing him to yelp with pain, to grab the pulsating member in both hands, and dance about in circles on one foot until the pain subsided. Since he ended up on his back on the barn floor, he used this opportunity to heap abuse on Flossie with some of his choicest epithets, as that beast, whose comprehension was nil and whose composure unassailable, went on chewing her cud with characteristic placidity.

When finally Angus got to his feet, his barn chores done for the time being, he began limping toward the doorway nursing his several hurts, itches and irritations as best he could. Thus engaged, and not fully attentive to his progress, he carelessly walked into a wooden pulley hanging in the barn doorway and blackened an eye. Suddenly his rage was exchanged for a surge of self-pity. He plopped down on a grassy knoll to surrender fully to the variety of aches and pains that wracked his body, only to arise rocket-like, propelled upward by that singular means of defense Yellow-jackets own.

Any person with a normal amount of sympathy could, at this point, sense the frustration that engulfed Angus. Feeling as if he should run and hide, he automatically started for the house where he knew that a well of sympathy could be drawn upon from his loving Bessie. But, he had taken no more than a few steps in this direction when he looked up to see the bull, having escaped from its pen, making off down the road at a brisk pace. Ignoring his battered condition, Angus took off promptly in full pursuit of this ornery beast, who when realizing that he was being chased, took a sudden left turn off the roadway into the neighbor's yard. Here he was soon entangled in the clothes lines, breaking them down, and scattering the lady's freshly hung wash high and low. Freed of this encumbrance, he next trampled on her rose garden, then left the scene through a wide hole he created in her picket fence, amidst the shrieks and protests of a woman gone mad.

Angus beat a hasty retreat knowing instinctively that he was no match for an hysterical woman. Once out of her earshot, he slowly and painfully headed homeward. He had a distance to travel, and, long before he got there, the neighbor lady was on the telephone giving Bessie McDuff "a piece of her mind." This, of course, alerted Bessie to what she might expect when her sore and angry husband arrived. She sat down on the sofa contemplating her situation. An irate husband she well knew was something to contend with. She had no fear of physical abuse, but was still extremely concerned about becoming the foil for Angus' ill-temper.

Bessie hadn't long to think. In a short time, the pathetic figure of Angus McDuff became visible approaching the house. What a sight he made limping badly, his one eye swelled half-shut, his face a picture of anger and frustration. If Bessie sees him coming she must certainly be shaking in her shoes. This was a man with a bag full of hostile feelings needing release; planning his entry, his statements, his actions; expecting a show of concern, a shower of sympathy, a flurry of attention.

Angus clomped into the washroom, bathed his hands and face with noisy splashings, applied antiseptic to his skinned arm, viewed his black eye in the mirror, took off his shirt and shook out the straw, ran a comb through his greying hair and entered the kitchen primed for the expected condolences of a loving wife. But the kitchen was empty of wife, of indication of meal preparation, of sound.

"Woman where are you?" he shouted surprised and newly aroused.

"I'm in here, dear," came the faint and plaintive reply from the direction of the bedroom. Moving to the bedroom door with more facility than seemed possible for a man in his sorry condition, ready to explode at his wife for her seeming indifference to his wants and needs, Angus was stopped short by the scene before him.

Lying on the bed in obvious distress, her hair in disarray, pale as a ghost with dark circles under her eyes, and emitting little cries of pain now and then as she clutched her breast was Bessie McDuff. Instantly concern showed on Angus' face. Before he knew it he was on his knees at bedside with Bessie's hand in his, earnestly inquiring the nature of her illness as his own miseries, his own anger evaporated. How quickly love can supercede hostility in crisis situations.

For the remainder of that day Angus gave tender attention to Bessie's needs. His considerations seemed the very thing to counteract her sudden illness. By night-fall she was able to leave her bed of pain for a chair in the living room, there to partake of nourishment kindly and inquisitively brought in by that very neighbor who had that very afternoon scoured Bessie's ears on the telephone. Seemingly news of Bessie's illness had tempered her feelings.

It is with joy that I report that by the next morning Bessie had miraculously recovered and resumed her daily duties as wife and housekeeper. This is a credit to her sturdy constitution.

Meanwhile, after returning home from her errand of kindness, Maude the neighbor lady, in conversation with her husband, Orville, surprisingly expressed certain opinions about Bessie's illness that I can only classify as slanderous and outrageous. No doubt there was an element of spite in these utterances springing from the incident with the bull, even though Angus had agreed to pay for all damages.

"Orville," said Maude, "I tell you that that woman was no more sick than I was." Fearing that her words were not impressing her husband and irked at the thought she protested in a loud voice. "Orville, You're Not Listening To A Word I'm Saying."

Orville who wasn't listening as usual gave his patented reply: "Yes, dear. You're absolutely right, dear," which often quieted her.

Apparently satisfied Maude continued.

"One look at her was all I needed to see that her face was covered with powder an inch thick, and the circles under her eyes were nothing but make-up. I intend, one of these days, to find out just what she was up to." Then she added disdainfully, "Men are such fools anyway."

"Fools," parroted Orville, having caught that one word in his annoyance at being distracted from the progress of the ball game on the radio.

A suspicious and mistrusting woman, this Maude, known far and wide for her catty comments and insinuating remarks. Maude should have her mouth taped shut as Orville has so many times wished. The very idea that Bessie, good soul that she is, would stoop to such deception is ridiculous--isn't it? You women are better judges of this than I. Let me know your opinions, please--between ball games, that is.

###############################

To stand still is to thwart progress. Not to progress is to die. But, what is progress? I know the dictionary says "forward movement". Still, is a taller building progress, or are two half its height? If a patient progresses in a hospital and recovers, but has lost a leg in the process, has he progressed? A city builds a community swimming pool because the river becomes polluted. Is there progress in that? A business man makes a million in crooked dealings. Can one progress backward? A kid progresses through school, but ain't learned much on the way. What kind of progress is that? Well, no use going on. Can't you now feel for me in my ignorance?

Some times progress has all the characteristics of a bully. It laughs at your protests and moves on. That telephone pole in your yard, those trees you lost when the road was widened, the piles of dirt left when the sewer was installed, the culvert that took away part of your lawn; all these things and more are done boldly in defiance of your wishes, and in the name of progress. Admit it, wouldn't you like to smash its pushy face once in a while?

###############################

The early morning sun was golden, and its rays split the eastern cloud-cover. It appeared to be raining flecks of gold as it shone upon the scattered snowflakes that were falling to rest on the somnolent earth. I felt an urge to rush outside with some manner of receptacle to catch as much as I could of this generous shower of wealth.

Then the snowflakes ceased falling, and the sun ducked behind a dark cloud. The golden flecks suddenly became pale, cold white dots against the green lawn, and my dreams of easy wealth were that quickly extinguished, replaced by the greyness of the changed panorama.

How many dreams of wealth, by how many hopefuls, have died as quickly.

MUSIC APPRECIATION

An abbreviated, unexpurgated history of music specifically designed for the secondary school.

Dedicated to my friends and colleagues, the music staff of Coopersville High School.

LESSON I   WIND INSTRUMENTS

Music was discovered by man in prehistoric times when a beatnik-type primordial man burped into a conch shell, and unintentionally sounded the note which millenniums later was called "A". Astonished at this accomplishment, this shaggy, evil-smelling ancestor of all musicians attempted to duplicate the belched "A" by intentionally blowing on the sea shell. For his effort he produced A flat, thereby doubling the musical knowledge of his day by lowering his first accomplishment one-half step, while simultaneously giving music a sense of direction.

Having in one matinee performance exhausted the musical range of this forerunner of the sound instruments, music history stood still for centuries. Actually there are surprisingly few variations of themes covering two notes. Thus music came to be a bore to primeval man. In addition musicians of this day were found to be tender morsels by the cannibalistic brotherhood, so eating one had the happy effect of relieving boredom and hunger at one and the same time. Of course, these circumstances threatened music with extinction.

LESSON II   VOCAL MUSIC

Like instrumental music, vocal music got its start unintentionally. It was in the same era that one of these early men, a hunter of great renown, captured a young dinosaur which he domesticated and trained to the extent that he, later on, after the beast reached maturity, was able to use it as a portable stairway by mastering the art of walking up the saw-toothed spines that grew along its back. In this way he was able to find food in places inaccessible to other cavemen. It was this sort of ingenuity that would one day bring on the Machine Age.

This mighty hunter had many female admirers--naturally, and their pursuit of him was thwarted time and again when he bashfully used the dinosaur's back as an escape route. Soon enough one beautifully muscled specimen of womanhood, whose desires were urgently compelling, pursued him up the bony stairway and had actually made her capture when she slipped, lost her balance, and began sliding down the serrated spine of the gigantic beast, unable to control her descent.

It was a great day for vocal music, for by the time this acme of early womanhood had reached the ground she had uttered all the notes in the musical scale including sharps and flats and with such clarity and purity of feeling as would not again be duplicated until the dawn of modern day opera.

As was the case with instrumental music a limitation appeared which thwarted the continued growth of this form of aesthetic expression. One hundred thousand years of "UG" and "UGH" songs, the only vocabulary of this age, again made music a dreary mode of expression.

LESSON III   PERCUSSION INSTRUMENTS

In the Umpah-pah River Valley millenniums ago there dwelt a tribe of savages who dearly loved a feast. They arranged to celebrate any event of consequence by gorging themselves with food and drink. Their beverage for these orgies of intemperance was an intoxicating potion brewed from the sap of the drum tree which had the effect of bulging bellies beyond belief while putting the imbibers in a trance-like state.

When the adult members of the tribe were all unconscious and lying inert upon the ground the tribal children played a kind of game of hopscotch by jumping on the bloated stomachs and bounding from one to the next.

When they tired of this activity they would sit down and slap the bulging abdomens of their drunken relatives with their hands or fists. This eventually developed into a rhythmical beat which when done with the right amount of force provoked a grunt of discomfort from the intoxicated person which followed the thumping sound of the slap on the stomach to create a boom-uph! boom-uph! sound which the children enjoyed producing in unison with one another.

It was a natural step forward when a teetotalling adult watching the children enjoy themselves by drumming on the protuberant abdomens of their drunken parents, out of feeling for the discomfort of adults generally, induced the children to pound on an animal skin stretched over a hollow log. The children were willing enough because the hollow log made a louder and more pleasant sound and could be beaten with more force than the crammed abdomens. This showed tone-consciousness.

When parents learned what had been happening to them during their stupor they readily constructed hollow log drums for their children and so it came to pass that the Umpah-pah River Valley was perpetually the home of drums and drummers.

LESSON IV   STRINGED INSTRUMENTS

The Combo Tribe of early men were considered to be a cult of mystics who invented and practised the earliest forms of sorcery. Uncivilized as they were, this cult never advanced beyond the rudimentary forms of mysticism, but their preoccupation with this satanic art was complete and all pervading.

The primary requirement upon each male tribal member was that upon reaching adulthood he should leave the village not to return until he had slain a sabre-toothed tiger, and was wearing its skin as a garment. Needless to say polygamy was practised within this tribe because many men left to face the ordeal of doing battle with this ferocious beast and few returned to become husbands and members of the cult.

One day adulthood came to Twang-Twang, a particularly chicken-hearted young man, who couldn't bring himself to kill a toad let alone a tiger. When he was forced out of the tribal community his chances of return seemed to be negative. However, after a few days of terror stricken pursuit of his quarry what should he chance upon but a freshly killed sabre-toothed tiger, badly clawed by its slayer, obviously another beast. Twang-Twang was so overjoyed at his good fortune that he lost his panic temporarily.

When Twang-Twang skinned his prize he found that the hide had been so badly shredded by the claws of its adversary that when donned as a garment it was no better cover than so many strings hanging down his back.

But Twang-Twang had proven his manhood. He had his tiger skin. It was difficult for him to draw himself into it because it was really an immature tiger who had worn this shredded skin in life.

After a struggle Twang-Twang encased himself in the skin of the beast which, as it dried in the sun, became more and more taut upon him until it finally had drawn so tightly that it humped his shoulder into an extremely uncomfortable position causing excruciating pain. To ease the pain Twang-Twang managed to work a wooden bowl he had carried with him in between the shredded hide and his own shoulders, which had the effect of forcing his shoulders into a more comfortable position.

Thus attired Twang-Twang headed for his village to be received into membership. As was customary, the entire village, having been alerted of his approach, stood ready to acclaim him as a hero and a tribal member. However, when he came near enough so that the sorry condition of his tiger skin garment could be seen his victorious return changed to amusement and ridicule, and an argument began to rage through the community about whether Twang-Twang had actually fulfilled the requirements for tribal membership by returning with a tiger skin which it was soon enough suspected had not been won in combat.

One voicing of this opinion seemed to convince all of the fact. A trial was demanded by general outcry and the man nearest grabbed Twang-Twang by the back of the shredded skin to force him along, but Twang-Twang lunged free, and the stretched gut snapped back into place as a vibrating string against a resonator, the wooden bowl supporting Twang-Twang's shoulders, creating a pleasant musical note which vibrated for a second or two, and which stopped all the jeering and accusing instantly. In the ensuing silence the string was plucked again by the same man, and as the mellow tone spiraled through the air a great shout of approval and appreciation went up from the gathered throng and all crowded up to Twang-Twang hoping to pluck the string themselves. The result was Twang-Twang was twanged for hours until he lost consciousness.

The trial was held. Twang-Twang was tried and found to be a liar, but music had advanced another step with the invention of the first stringed instrument. It is immaterial that the word liar became corrupted in later years, and is now spelled "lyre."

LESSON V   CONDUCTING

The history of conducting is a simple story--almost unbelievable. The day had to come when the conch shell artist, the hollow-log drummer, the stringed liar (later spelled "lyre") player, and the vocalist all met at Combo in the Umpah-pah River Valley during inter-tribal high level conference arranged to discuss, not music, but war.

When evening came and the convening chiefs relaxed from their day of bargaining, the musicians broke out their instruments and began entertaining individually. The clash of tempos and melodies resulted in a cacophony of sound that irritated the listeners, one of whom was subject to epileptic seizures, and who suddenly became the victim of one of these attacks. As the seizure overcame him, he jumped to his feet, flailing his arms wildly, swinging his head forward and backward until his hair stood on end, distorting his features, rocking back and forth on his heels, and barking out staccato sounds.

The seizure lasted only about sixty seconds, but when the unfortunate victim of the attack lapsed into unconsciousness the musicians were playing in complete harmony.

The value of a conductor in music was thus established, but for centuries thereafter musical groups played only when under the leadership of a man in the throes of a fit. Today conductors have learned to simulate these seizures so musical groups can perform at any time.

###################################

I swear, there exists on earth no body of pent up water, however large or small, willing to accept its present condition as permanent. Restlessness is its outstanding characteristic. It is continually and eternally seeking outlet, impatient for movement. Once an escape route is located, however minute, it employs itself feverishly on its enlargement. Drips become trickles, trickles become gushes, and gushes become torrents as it moves on to its next place of imprisonment, there to repeat its search for escape. What, you ask, provoked this observation? Our */!@ kitchen sink sprung a leak, that's what.

1977   LET JUSTICE PREVAIL

He was a hunter in whom the pleasure of hunting stirred primitive emotions. He was a big game hunter who thrilled in the chase and excelled in the kill. He was an intrepid hunter who feared no beast and stalked the largest and fiercest with thirty-ought-thirty courage. When he went hunting it was with the certain knowledge that all the odds were stacked in his favor, and the possibility of the unexpected happening was as far removed as the purchase of the latest and best equipment could make it. His rifle, now slung over his shoulder, is a powerful weapon of incredible range and firing power. His aim of this piece is greatly enhanced by a scope attached. In a leather case at his side is a pair of binoculars capable of enlarging his range of vision by several powers of magnification. His vehicle laughs at rough terrain and outruns the swiftest animals.

Thus equipped, we discover our hunter on the plains of Africa, dreadfully upset and cursing the circumstance that has emptied the landscape of game. We observe him, in his frustration, park his vehicle and set off walking, and hear him mutter, "where in hell are ya!" Trudging on, his ruffled thoughts goad him to greater exasperation, and he expostulates further with even more vehemence, "this is a waste of time, I might better have stayed in bed!" This followed by a few choice vituperations hurled at the emptiness to assault our ears, and we are somewhat inclined to reduce our respect for him as a person. The hunter is but a gun carrier when no game is to be seen, and our hunter's unhappiness seems understandable and we are duly sympathetic.

Keeping close, we can almost see his discouragement grow as time passes. "Where are ya anyway," he shouts at nothing, as nothing in the line of game is visible. Soon, evidently surrendering to circumstance, he ceases walking, finds a grassy slope and sits himself down. Continuing to watch, we see him unleash his binoculars, scan the horizon all around, return them to their pouch, pull a can of beer from his jacket, gulp it down and throw the empty can at the nothingness with such violence that we grow apprehensive about his mental attitude, and recede a few paces to insure our safety.

A slight rest and he appears somewhat calmed. We then observe him unsling his rifle, eye it with admiration, pat it affectionately, and begin to aim it through use of its scope. Suddenly we realize that he is imagining targets non-existent in the landscape. We read his thoughts as he aims here and there to down a lion, a buffalo, a rhinoceros, a leopard in that order while cluttering the empty horizon with their carcasses. We believe he is next to fell a dragon that has loomed up in his fantasy, when, amazingly, he ceases this wholesale slaughter, much to our relief, and with our wholehearted approval. All this slaughter without expending a single shot from his expensive rifle must be some kind of record kill.

We begin to think better of him as he lays his gun on the ground, goes to each supposed carcass, stands beside it in a triumphant pose, and is photographed by a photographer he conjures up for that very purpose. And we give him a good mark for tidiness when he clears the area of dead beasts and dissolves the photographer before returning to his rifle.

My, oh my! Wouldn't you know! As he nears the slope where his gun rests, we see him stop suddenly and draw back as if surprised. He is staring in disbelief, and we see why. His rifle is now entwined in the coils of a colorful poisonous snake that is making threatening motions with its head, as if asserting ownership, and ready to defend its claim. In this predicament, our fearless hunter, we are shocked to observe, is displaying a surprising timidity. For a brief time he stands immobilized as if unsure what he might do about the outright and flagrant usurping of his private property. Next we see him make a few threatening gestures at the snake, shout invective in its direction, toss a few hands full of sand at it, all with no better result than to make the snake more possessive of its claim to ownership and even more ready to defend it.

Unexpectedly, we realize that our fearless hunter, now disarmed, has come to a hasty decision. We observe him throw up his arms in complete despair, shout a vile curse at the sky and begin walking slowly toward his vehicle. We are ashamed of him when we can only admit to ourselves that he has ceded ownership of that expensive weapon to the snake without benefit of legalities or exchange of currency. Our estimation of him drops sharply in the face of his cowardice.

Contrarily, the snake is obviously well satisfied that it has made a good bargain. As we watch we see the new owner investigate its prize more closely. An attempt to crawl down the gun barrel failing, we see it dart its pointed head into the metal loop that houses the trigger causing the rifle to fire. Our hunter, in his orgy of killing imaginary beasts, had foolishly laid down his rifle cocked, a fatal error. The gun is pointed directly at the broad back of our retreating hunter and the bullet finds its mark. Down he falls, instantly relieved of all earthly cares, to become the one and only actual fatality in the entire surroundings. We are stunned by its suddenness and can only remark that such carelessness with deadly weapons has cost many a hunter his life.

Dead men, it is said, tell no tales, but there are those who, with their detective skills, can reconstruct from the evidence what actually happened. A search party sent out the next day to locate the missing hunter finds the body without difficulty and sets about determining what happened to cause his death. That he has been shot in the back being obvious, they carefully trace the path of the bullet, discover the rifle, and to their amazement, the snake also dead, with its head fatally pinched between the trigger of the rifle and the metal loop that housed it. A short parley and they have the solution, but what they agree has happened is too incredible to relate with any expectation of belief. This upsets them noticeably.

"You can report it," says one to the other.

"Oh, no!" replies the second, "You're in charge, you report it."

"What will the Park Ranger say when I tell him it is a case of a hunter being shot with his own rifle by a snake?" asks the first. "Would you believe such a report if you were the Ranger?" he asks.

"Well," says the second, "you'll need to be convincing, but that is your job, not mine."

"Just be sure you back me up in my report," says the first as they leave the scene.

The Park Ranger has the expected reaction. "Don't joke with me," he says sternly, "this is a serious matter."

But, when his two subordinates stick to their story and corroborate one another beyond doubting, the Park Ranger goes out to check for himself. Convinced, he in turn is overcome with a similar feeling of embarrassment as he considers the necessity of relaying such an incredible story to the legal authorities and would gladly have avoided doing so, had he a way.

The Coroner, a man hardened in the knowledge of life's many exitings, is not overly impressed when informed. "Humph!" he says, "that's a new one on me," and records the details in his Obituary Book with the same flourish of pen as he would any other person's death.

At this point, the Park Ranger, alert to possible repercussions fearing that knowledge of the cause of death might induce some overly cause-minded citizen's group to demand the extermination of all snakes in the park, asks that the strange manner of our hunter's death be kept from the public. To this the Coroner agrees, but the winds of gossip have a way of blowing in receptive ears, and in a day or two the whole story becomes public knowledge.

"Gun-toting Snake Kills Hunter" blares one headline of a newspaper. "Garden of Eden Episode Avenged" shrills another. The result was a barrage of cruel jokes and demeaning remarks that, had our hunter been living, would have been humiliating to him, and could have made him fearful of showing his face in public.

Among Womenfolk there exists a belief that it is their cruel lot in life to suffer for their Menfolk's misdeeds and shortcomings. This seems clearly borne out in this instance. The wife of our late hunter, a high-strung woman, having swooned on receiving news of her husband's death, having wept convulsively at his funeral, is presently at home under sedation, in a perilous state of health and under a doctor's care. The poor thing hated guns, secretly contributed to an Anti-gun Society, couldn't bear to listen to her husband's hunting tales, had often expressed her revulsion of the stuffed heads that hung on the walls of his den, and has been quoted as having said: "They stare at me and are impossible things to dust." Of course she only voiced these opinions to female friends, having ever been, in some degree, afraid of her husband.

Here now, some six months after the funeral, we find her somewhat recovered from her ordeal and longing for the security and companionship she had know so long. It is then she impulsively accepts a proposal of marriage tendered by a long standing acquaintance and becomes his bride in a private ceremony. Regrettable to relate, this was helpful to her, but her problems were not destined to evaporate that easily. Located a short distance from the white community in which she resided was a village of Pygmies, long established, who revered the snake and had for centuries worshiped them. In their primitive beliefs, to kill a snake was an unpardonable sin, but to be killed by a snake elevated the victim to Godlike stature.

While it is recorded fact that until the death of our hunter no white man had ever been considered eligible for this honor, the unusual circumstances surrounding his death were seen by these miniature people as support for their belief that the snake became a reincarnation of the person it killed. This, they reasoned, had nothing whatsoever to do with a man's color or eligibility for a place in their pantheon of worshiped gods. So it was decided by general agreement to extend this high honor to our dead hunter. This, you can be certain, boded no good for his fragile wife.

The Pygmy conclave, therefore, was soon busy in preparation for a great "Celebration of the Snake" to take place on a date selected by their Chief, Papatonga. First it was necessary that huge quantities of combustibles be gathered and piled high in the center of the compound; birds with colored feathers must be snared to provide colorful headdresses; certain plants sought for, gathered and extracted of their juices as pigments for body colors; and other plants, berries and fruits for preparing the native intoxicating beverage called "Azooba". These activities went on for two weeks and when all was in readiness, Chief Papatonga set the date for the Celebration of the Snake as of the first night of the dark moon. Anticipation ran high among the Pygmies, such celebrations being so rare that one in a lifetime was the most one could hope to participate in. When the appointed day dawned, Chief Papatonga made preparation by waddling down to the river where he bathed.

For a number of years these two nearby settlements had existed in an harmonious relationship. The whites had, with benevolent condescension, provided their backward neighbors with all their disposables in charitable fashion, hoping thereby to raise their level of living, and had been most obliging in sharing with them all their epidemics and vices. The Pygmies had, in return accepted these rewards good naturedly, without in any way changing their long established customs, making use of what was given them in ways never intended, and in some instances with a kind of ingenuity that surprised their donors, and led some whites to regard them as human beings.

With these magnanimous attitudes existing, when the whites were invited to attend the Celebration of the Snake, a good delegation accepted, arriving in a body just as the huge bonfire lighted the evening sky to signal the beginning of the celebration. Soon caught up in the convivial spirit of the occasion and rendered quite free of their usual feelings of prejudice by the potency of the Azooba supplied to them, they arrived at the state of genuine compatibility, which evokes the observation that Azooba drinking may be the true pathway to racial equality.

Beginning with dancing around the bonfire, proceeding to individual feats of strength, on to gorging on the delicacies prepared for the occasion, and of course Azooba quaffing at all stages of the preliminaries, the occasion seemed to be nicely building up to the climactic finale, awaited eagerly by all. This was, of course, the apotheosizing of the white hunter of our tale.

This being a serious and somber ritual, when the time came the audience quieted quickly and began seating themselves before a rude platform erected for the occasion. It seemed that to seat a mortal killed by a snake among the select gods required incantations of a dreary sort, the mixing and drinking of magic potions concocted by the tribal Witch Doctor, the careful handling of a snake of good size trapped for the ceremony; and for its denouement, the actual sacrifice of the snake to become the conveyor of the dead hunter's spirit to enthronement in the Great Beyond. All this accomplished by Chief Papatonga with the assistance of the Witch Doctor.

The widow of our dead hunter, being the honored guest at this ceremony, all but forced to attend lest she appear indifferent to her late husband's memory, and under strong pressure from the leaders of the white community, who feared her absence might adversely effect the existing good relationship between the two villages, endured it all, being a non-drinker, in a state of sobriety. To say that she became terrified by these revolting proceedings would be to put it mildly. To know that she had the added fear that somehow this ceremony might, in its process, restore her dead husband to life would better reveal the true depth of her suffering and anguish.

Refusing cup after cup of azooba, which she might better have drunk to calm her whirling emotions, she managed somehow to remain conscious throughout the entire proceedings, glued like a statue to her seat. That she had to be carried away at the conclusion of the ceremony, babbling like one insane, caught the attention of very few, and registered no lasting impression on any.

This singular event, ranked among the all time highlights of tribal history by that eminent historian Chief Papatonga, was later described more accurately by the Witch Doctor to a bevy of reporters. Waving his arms energetically and speaking with great fervor, he said, "Momboola lamamsa tusa compoli itsa altootze, azooba, azooba, azooba!", which interpreted meant, "whites, pygmies, they all make me sick! Drunks! Drunks! Drunks!"

It was perhaps a fortnight later when Chief Papatonga, who loved the limelight and delighted in ceremony, announced a new honor for the already tortured, newly married and barely recovered widow. He would, he announced through the press, make her a special presentation from his grateful community. Again refusal seemed impossible. The Press featured the coming event with pictures of the two principals and rated it as vital to inter-community relations. Under this duress, the bereaved one had no escape, although the mere thought of it upset her badly, aggravating her already delicate condition; not that she could presume with any right that this occasion would be like the former one, or had any foreknowledge of what the award might be. She put her reliance in sedatives and anxiously waited.

The day of the ceremony approaching, the pitiful lady grew more and more apprehensive, and her imaginings more fanciful. "With what am I to be presented?" she asked. Her concerned new husband tried valiantly to calm her, and quiet her fears with suggestions ranging from rare edibles to a pot of gold to little effect. It became a trying period for both.

At last came the day, a civic highlight. Chief Papatonga and a delegation of his tribal members marched to the white settlement and directly to the main square where he was warmly greeted by a similar group of whites. Filling the square was a crowd of citizens from both communities. The necessary formalities accomplished and over, Chief Papatonga, with pomposity and gesticulation favored with a short speech in his native language, little understood by the whites present, but loudly applauded none-the-less. He then indicated that he wished the honored guest to advance, which she did being supported by her husband. When she was in place, standing before the Chief, he turned to a tribesman behind him, opened a basket being held by him, and took from it the intended award. Turning again to face the recipient, with a face that pictured his pleased feelings and with a tenderness that would have become a courtier, standing on tiptoes because of his inferior height, with a flourish, draped about the shoulders of the honoree the skin of the snake sacrificed at the previous ceremony.

Whatever it was that caused it, the recipient was beset with a sudden weakness of the knees. Her alert husband sprang to her aid, supported her in her difficulty, steered her limp hand into the hand of Chief Papatonga as an expression of thanks, walked her out of the square in a decorous manner leaving the Chief smiling broadly, immensely pleased and diverted by the attention focused on him by photographers and reporters.

Once free of the crowd, the distraught lady crumpled into a boneless mass of flesh. Carried home and laid in bed, she was in a comatose state for twenty four hours thereafter, only to rouse out of this perilous condition, clutching wildly at her shoulders while shrieking in terror, "get that damned thing off me!" and again falling into a coma.

Hovering around her bedside, her concerned husband sought to restore her spirits with a pat on the arm, words of comfort, a kiss on the forehead and a gentle fanning of her face, all remedies not much credited in medical books. When at last she revived looking pale and disheveled, shuddering at intervals and moaning between times, even we in our unprofessional opinion had to admit that the probability of her eventual recovery lay in the realm of serious doubt.

The arrival of her physician was a relief to the worried husband. After checking over the patient he consulted with the husband. His professional opinion termed the patient's condition "grave". He left medicines, announced he would return on the morrow, and left.

The husband returned to his wife's bedside, noticed how poorly she looked and his concern grew accordingly. He finds her at the moment awake and lucid, but fretting over a new concern.

"My husband," she begins-

"I'm here beside you, dear," he responds sweetly.

"No! No!" she says with vexation "I mean my dear dead husband."

"Oh," says he, obviously disappointed.

"My dead husband," she starts again, "is now all alone," and she wails piteously.

"What do you mean, dearest - all alone?" he asks.

"I mean, he's the only white man in a black heaven," she answers and wails again. "I just know he's terribly lonesome for me. I must go to him. I hear him calling for me," she adds as she suddenly sits bolt upright in bed, utters an unearthly scream, falls back on her pillow and is gone.

Well, there you have our story as we beheld it from beginning to end. We suppose it qualifies as a tragedy, although it had its humorous aspects. Call it what you will, it's not an everyday happening you must agree.

Before we part ways, we stand for a time discussing the events that have held our attention for the past several weeks. Snakes having been indirectly the cause of the deaths of our two principals, the hunter and his wife, we enter into a tirade against them, which calls forth our most scathing, contemptuous, reviling, loathsome adjectives, we are going at it hot and heavy when we are startled by a voice saying.

"You are being most unfair, you know."

"And who might you be?" we ask.

"Call me a fair-minded person who, having heard you revile snakes without any consideration whatsoever given to the snake's side of the issue, felt impelled to state the obvious, you are being unfair."

"Are you inferring that you would defend snakes?" we ask.

"Yes, I would in this instance," was his reply. "Someone should," he adds.

"So we are unfair, are we?" we respond. "Are you aware that we have been witness to two recent deaths, both attributed to those loathsome creatures? Being aware of that, yet you would defend them?"

"I repeat, in the interest of fairness, yes, I would defend them."

"You then would hold the right of snakes over and above those of humans? Is that what you are saying?"

"No! No! You misunderstand me. All I am interested in is fairness. Both sides of an issue should be heard and the matter settled on the basis of evidence supplied."

"Now you sound like a lawyer. What would you have us do, set up court and hold a trial?"

"That would be the ideal way to resolve the issue. Yes, if you are willing, that is what I would suggest."

"Are we then to suppose you have a snake handy who speaks the language, and can defend itself?"

"There's the problem. Snakes cannot speak for themselves. Would you consider me the snake and allow me to state its case?"

"We are strongly inclined to answer that request in a way you would resent, but we won't. If you wish to go that far to defend snakes, yes, we'll go along. But who is to decide the case?"

"We'll need a judge, that's true. Look, isn't that Chief Papatonga ambling this way? Would you accept him as the judge?"

"Why yes, I respect the Chief's good sense."

"All right then, I'll acquaint him with the circumstances and invite him to be our arbiter." This the stranger does, and the Chief, flattered by the invitation, accepts readily. He seats himself on a nearby log, and is ready to perform his duty.

"Now, Your Honor," begins the stranger, "our friends here," and he indicates me, "will state the case for the prosecution. I will then, in rebuttal, defend the snake against their charges. At the conclusion, you, Chief will be expected to render a verdict. Do you understand your role?"

"Yes, yes," replies the Chief. "I've served in this capacity many times in tribal disputes. I understand, and I am ready. Proceed."

"Very well," says the stranger, then turning to me announces, "all is ready for you to begin."

Begin I did and before I ended I had laid out an airtight case that should surely indict the snake beyond escaping. My group was pleased with my performance and so, I thought, was the Chief, who had listened with interest and several times nodded his head as if agreeing with what I had said.

Judge -   "I now call upon the counsellor for the defense to state his case."

Counsellor -   "Thank you, Your Honor. With your permission I will proceed by questioning the defendant whose role I will assume, thereby hoping to establish its position toward the indictment."

Judge -   "Proceed."

Counsellor -   "You are a snake, a member of the reptilian order, are you not?"

Snake -   "I am."

Counsellor -   "You are here in court charged in the deaths of two human beings. Do you understand the charge?"

Snake -   "You refer to the hunter and his wife, I presume."

Counsellor -   "Yes."

Snake -   "Yes, I understand the charge."

Counsellor -   "How then do you plead to the charge, guilty or not guilty?"

Snake -   "Not guilty!"

Counsellor -   "Am I to understand that you plead not guilty in the face of evidence, already presented by the prosecution, that you were observed to have fired the rifle that killed the hunter, which set in motion a chain of events leading to the death of his wife?"

Snake -   "That is correct."

Counsellor -   "Let me understand. You are not denying the charges brought against you, yet you are declaring yourself not guilty. How can that be?"

Snake -   "In the first place, the very idea of putting me on trial here is ridiculous. There is no precedent for such a trial, I am a snake being tried in a court conducted by humans, to be tried under human laws for an alleged crime against humans. This whole procedure is a farce. It's unjust!"

Counsellor -   "That's all very well, but you have not answered my question. In the face of facts to the contrary, how can you possibly plead not guilty?"

Snake -   "By reason of being a snake."

Judge -   "This is unacceptable unless the defendant can explain its reasoning better than it has so far."

Counsellor -   "You have heard the judge. Tell us by what reasoning you persist in pleading not guilty."

Snake -

"Well, to begin with, let me take you back to the Garden of Eden. You will recall that it was there that one of my kind inveigled Eve to defy the edict of God and eat fruit from the forbidden tree. It was there, in retaliation, that a wrathful God sentenced all snakes to be forever cursed, to crawl upon their bellies and eat dust and put enmity between snakes and humans forever."

Counsellor -

"Yes, that is well known, but-"

Snake -

"I haven't finished. Must I be interrupted?"

Counsellor -

"Sorry. Proceed."

Snake -

"From that day forward snakes have been branded evil creatures. From evil creatures the expectation must be evil deeds. In other words, when a snake commits an evil act it is doing what it should be expected to do. What is a right action for a snake cannot be declared a crime. Of what then am I guilty?"

Counsellor -

"What you are saying then is that under human laws you are guilty of the crimes with which you are charged, but because you are a snake, not a human being, these laws do not apply to your case and you are not guilty under laws that apply to snakes?"

Snake -

"Precisely!"

Counsellor -

"Your Honor, I rest my case, and await your verdict."

Judge -

"Not guilty. Court adjourned."

############################

Today, the individual has more "Rights" be he upstanding or criminal, than he can properly keep in mind; this due in large part to exhaustive explorations into the Constitution's lack of specificity, and to the legal system's remarkable ability to uncover their intentions and meanings that could conceivably be causing grave-turnings on the parts of its illustrious authors.

This causes me to wonder why some enterprising person has not yet seen fit to produce a handy Compendium of Rights to be carried on one's person for ready consultation and sure recognition of violations, with pertinent advice for rectification in suits-at-law. I am inclined to believe our Rights are being treaded upon almost daily. Think of the monetary loss to abused individuals this represents.

Should you appropriate my suggestions, and assemble such a Compendium, I caution you, do not anywhere within its covers be so naive as to mention the word "obligations". To do so would most certainly brand you as a rag picker in the dump heap of discredited and discarded notions.

1954   VANDER VANDER THE ALL DUTCHMAN

(Editor's note: This story was written for the Students of Coopersville High School.)

During the last two weeks I have reported to you a strange and unexplained event which occurred seemingly without reason. You will recall that I was visited by a huge ghost-like figure of a man wearing wooden shoes who handed me a cup of orange-gold color and said, "This is where I think it belongs." Before I could get over my fright and question the specter he had vanished completely, but the cup was still in my hand and very real. Later a phone call advised me to search for the answer to the riddle of the ghost and the cup, which I did. After much trouble and time I had the good fortune to come across an ancient manuscript which I felt certain contained the secret I was looking for. But the work of translating it required time, and only now can I read you my translation just completed. It is, I assure you, a tale well calculated to confound the dense. This is the story as I have deciphered it.

Between the Yellow Sea and the Red Sea, where the waters of the two mix and blend, is the Orange sea, a little known body of water seldom heard of in this part of the world. In fact, some say that it has disappeared entirely in recent years after a soft drink factory was located on its shores.

Many strange tales are told about the Orange Sea, and one of the most interesting is that concerning the Magic Cup. As it is told, the course of a sailing vessel captained by Vander Vander, the All-Dutchman, led into the Orange Sea. In the hold of this proud ship was a cargo of the finest wooden shoes ever made, and on board was the greatest firebug, arsonist, that is, in all the history of the Netherlands. His presence was, of course, unknown to Vander Vander, the All-Dutchman, who would have had him strung up to the yardarm had he suspected.

With all these wooden shoes in the hold of the ship you can well imagine how the firebug had itched to get his hands on a match. Unfortunately matches had not yet been invented so his burning desire was nipped in the bud, thwarted, that is.

When this good ship, captained by Vander Vander, the

All-Dutchman, with its hold filled with the finest wooden shoes ever made, sailed into the Orange Sea the arsonist could no longer restrain his desire to start a fire. With a frenzy of effort, spurred on by the color of the Orange Sea, which whipped his criminal tendency into a mania, the firebug rubbed two wooden shoes together so hard and so fast that they caught on fire from the friction, and in no time at all set the entire ship ablaze.

Vander Vander, the All-Dutchman was equal to the emergency. Being of prodigious strength and uncommon intelligence, he ripped planks from the deck of the doomed ship with his bare hands, fashioned a crude raft, and ordered his crew to abandon ship to the safety of the raft. This accomplished and all hands safe, Vander Vander, the All-Dutchman returned to the burning ship to save the most prized of all his possessions, a drab looking gold cup which was used on all the ships he captained as a drinking cup. It's magic qualities were the thing that made him risk his life to save it.

Outstanding about the magic properties of this cup was its unique ability to come out free and clean after being dipped into a barrel of the foulest drinking water imaginable, and you can well imagine how foul the drinking water became on sailing ships many months out of port. Often the water crawled with tiny creatures and reeked of staleness.

After he had recovered the Magic Cup, Vander Vander, the All-Dutchman leaped into the Orange Sea and swam mightily for shore. Being a powerful man with muscles of steel and the endurance of an ox he reached the shore after several hours and in time made his way back to the land of dikes and windmills where he was greeted as a national hero and posed for many statues, but an unusual thing had happened to the Magic Cup. The hours in the Orange Sea had stained it a color which could only be called orange-gold, and which no manner of wiping could remove. In fact, Vander Vander the All-Dutchman was himself like-wise stained, and so permanently that his descendants became known as the House of Orange, as history books will confirm.

For many years Vander Vander, the All-Dutchman lived in honor with his countrymen who considered the Orange-Gold Magic Cup to be one of their national treasures, and its good luck quality made it world famous. It is claimed that Columbus touched it and sailed to discover America, that Wellington rubbed it before he won at Waterloo, and that Dirk Dyksterhouse brushed against it and scored 62 goals in one game of ice hockey. The Magic Cup performed many feats of magic, that is until the flood when it was lost forever, or so it seemed. The flood occurred one day when the dutch boys were counting in arithmetic class and there wasn't a free finger to plug the dike.

As I reported to you recently, a cup was left in my office by a huge ghost-like man wearing wooden shoes who said to me, "This is where I think this belongs." Naturally, I did not understand the significance or the apparition of the cup at the time, but now that I have come across this lost page of history I begin to see that the huge ghost-like figure who appeared before me was Vander Vander, the All-Dutchman, and the cup which he left in my office is none other than the long lost Orange-Gold Magic Cup. The words that he uttered now take on a wonderful significance. How can I think otherwise than that Vander Vander, the All-Dutchman, having found the lost cup, has chosen our school as the place of honor and has entrusted the keeping of it to us.

I am sure that each of you would like to share in the good luck properties of this magic cup which once was the property of Vander Vander, the All-Dutchman. To make this possible it will be awarded each week from now on to the home room which has the highest percentage of attendance. Your home room teachers will tell you how it will be possible for your home room to get possession of it and its magic properties. I hope you get it soon and that it brings you the good luck it has brought others. As far as I know this is the only school in the world with such a trophy, and I hope that the Student Council or some other group will take it upon themselves to tell the freshman each year the story of Vander Vander the All-Dutchman until it becomes as much a part of our school as the school colors. A sort of a tradition.

##############################

Who am I to fault Cupid? Yet, if his assigned purpose is to inspire love and romance, who couldn't second guess some of the ridiculous pairings he makes? And who doesn't believe that, could he filch Cupid's arrows he could fling them with better result.

Consider the present divorce rate; shouldn't one assume that his shafts are falling out of hearts, as love dies? Or suggest that the little fellow's bow-bending arm has tired from long use? Or conclude that he is now shooting blunted shafts?

Why then hasn't he been replaced? I suspect he has a union contract myself.

1982   WHAT IS THIS THING CALLED LOVE?

"Happy Valentine's Day", said my mother as she got me out of bed one winter's morning to go to school. "Here are some valentines I bought at the 10¢ store for you to give to your friends," she added as she handed them to me. "You can sign them and give them to whomever you wish. Now hurry and get dressed," was her parting direction as she kissed me and headed back downstairs.

This wasn't my first Valentine's Day, you understand; but it was the first one in my young life that had significance. I dawdled over dressing, then sat on the edge of my bed looking at each valentine with great interest. Each had a picture of a heart pierced by an arrow, obviously flung from the drawn bow of a chubby character identified as Cupid, who did not, in my estimation, look the part. To me, he looked to be a fat kid in diapers, old enough, I thought, to have been toilet-trained long ago.

Next I checked each one of the hearts on the valentines for signs of bleeding--I was a stickler for realism--but found none. This disappointed me considerably. Then, wondering how anyone's heart could be separated from one's body for shootin' purposes, I felt suddenly overwhelmed with questions needing answers. I read the verses on the back side of each valentine. All ended in "I love you." "What mush!" I thought to myself. Then I began to worry about having to hand them out to my friends, and was really bothered by the thought that they might think I meant what the valentines said.

I walked to school that day, undecided whether I would hand them out or not. Half way there, here came Josephine barreling down on me at full speed. Josephine was a girl I always hoped to avoid because she had buck teeth and was always a huggin' me. Since it was too late to escape her onslaught this time, I decided to ask her some of the questions I had on my mind. Josephine was a year older than me. Josephine knew a lot about love. This I could testify to, being her principal victim as I was.

Before I could say a word, she floored me with a question of her own, "Are you going to give me a valentine?" she asked with her tongue hanging out in anticipation of a favorable answer. Well, I wasn't agoing to, but under the circumstances with her arm around my neck, what else could I do but assent? I said: "yes" in a way that would have wounded the feelings of a more sensitive girl, but pleased Josephine who hugged me tighter. Josephine was really strong for a girl. I ducked out of her clutches and asked:

"Say, Josephine, who is Cupid?"

"Don't you know that?" she laughed, "why, he's the God of Love," and as you may have guessed, squeezed me harder.

Just then, Melvin ran up to us. Melvin liked Josephine, I suppose because they both had buck teeth. Melvin hit me with his fist and ran off. Josephine kissed my cheek where it was scuffed and shouted unkind things after Melvin as he fled. As I pushed myself away from Josephine's attentions, I wondered why it was that Josephine liked me, who didn't like her, and didn't like Melvin, who did.

I wasn't much hurt and I had more questions to ask Josephine, so I did. "If Cupid is a god, is he a poor god?" I asked next.

"Why?" she asked me. "What do you mean?"

"I mean, can't he afford any clothes?"

"Oh!" she replied in a giggly manner, "that's just the way gods go around. They never wear clothes."

"They don't!" I said in great surprise, puzzled by the thought of it being winter and all. After digesting this bit of information, I asked:

"Is Cupid a he or a she?"

This seemed to stump her momentarily. Finally she said "I think he's a he but--!" Here she acted kinda embarrassed before getting out, "Who can tell. I never saw him undressed."

"Oh!" I said in my innocence, imagining that were he undressed, that information would be printed across his belly on a ribbon.

"Why does he shoot arrows into hearts?" I asked next.

"That's 'cause when you get shot by Cupid you fall in love," was her knowing response as she put her face so close to mine that her teeth looked like a piano keyboard. If I hadn't ducked just in the nick of time I think she would'a kissed me. This probability made me squeamish, so I ran for school with this new information circulatin' through my head; information, that I got directly from--should I be honest and say--the horse's mouth? As I ran, the thought struck me that falling in love and fightin' Indians exposed one to the same danger from arrows.

I distributed my valentines, and got returns. I didn't give one to Melvin because he hit me with his fist and I didn't get to hit him back. So I gave that one to Josephine, who seemed overly pleased to get it. She leaned over from her desk, and in hot breath, whispered to me that she felt like she had been shot by Cupid's arrow. Guessin' what that meant for me was more squeezin', I decided on the spot to run all the way home after school. Worse for me, I got one back from Josephine with X's all over it. I also got one from Melvin with the "I love you" changed to read "I hate you." When I didn't give Melvin one back, he stuck out his tongue at me and had to stay after school. This evened things up between us for the day.

For the rest of Valentine's Day, I went around walking backwards and turning circles so Cupid couldn't get a good shot at me.

What I had learned from Josephine didn't come near answering all my questions, so, once home, I said to my mother, "Ma, if I give someone a valentine, does that mean I hafta love them?"

"Not necessarily," she answered without payin' much attention to me, exceptin' to add in a cross tone of voice "I wish you'd stop that walking backwards! Why are you doing that anyway?".

When I told her why, she laughed so hard I was hurt in my feelings. "What's so funny about that?" I asked petulantly.

"Nothing! I guess," she answered, as she turned back to her work, still chuckling and sayin' over her shoulder, "I never know what to expect from you". "Maybe not," I thought, "but you ain't been much help so far."

"Ma," I said then, "have you ever seen Cupid?"

I could see she was gittin' a little peeved with me, but she answered me. "Of course not, she said, "No one has ever seen the real Cupid. He's just a fictitious character. Now will you begone somewhere. Can't you see I'm busy," this said in a tone of voice I recognized as final.

"Can I go to Grandpa's house then?" I asked.

"I wish you would!" she replied, as if the thought of being

rid of me was pleasin' to her. So I headed for Grandpa's house.

Along the way I met Jason. "What luck," I thought, "Jason can tell me anything I wanta know." To me, Jason had been a regular oracle. I stopped him and said,

"Say, Jason, My Ma told me that Cupid was a 'fikitous character'. What does fikitous mean?"

"Whatdya say?" asked Jason.

"Fikitous character," I repeated. "What does that mean?"

"Oh," said Jason, who then went immediately into deep thought. Next he repeated the word fikitous two or three times before he asked, "How do you spell that?"

"I don't know," I said. "Like it sounds,I guess."

"Oh, sure!" said Jason. "That means 'crazy!'"

"Thanks, Jason," I said, in envy of his vast knowledge.

Leaving Jason and continuing on, I thought about this, and began to make more sense to me. If, as Ma had said, Cupid was a fikitous character and fikitous meant crazy, then I could better account for his goin' around bare naked in winter, shootin' arrows at hearts, and spreadin' that mush called love. My admiration for Jason grew accordingly.

Further along my way I came upon Wilma. I said "hello" to Wilma very sweetly, because Wilma was very pretty, and had never once tried to hug me--which I wished she had. Wilma didn't stop to chat--she never seemed to want to. "Why?" I wondered, comparing her disinclination with Josephine's eagerness. This whole love business grew more and more confusing to me. Thinkin' how nice it would be to be hugged by Wilma, while walking backwards, I bumped into a tree and bruised the back of my head.

With my thoughts a'pilin' up and my mind a whirlin', I arrived at Grandpa's house. The fact that Grandpa was a sour old curmudgeon, whose marriage had ended in disaster, and whose attitudes were pickled in pessimism, probably made him the wrong person to consult. After the usual greetings, I said to Grandpa:

"Grandpa, did you ever get shot by Cupid's arrow?" Grandpa eyed me suspiciously as if judgin' whether my question deserved an answer, saw my serious face and said bitterly,

"Yes. That little devil got me in a weak moment."

"Did it hurt?" I continued, lookin' up into his face.

Grandpa thought a minute before sayin', "No, it felt good at the time."

"Do you still have the arrow in your heart?" I asked next. This caused him to frown forbiddingly. "Why are you askin' me all these questions?" he snapped. "Things like that shouldn't concern a young shaver like you for several years yet."

"Oh!" I responded, greatly relieved to learn that I wasn't yet fair game for Cupid's arrow. "How old were you, Grandpa, when you got shot?"

"Old enough to know better," he answered sourly while makin' a wry face.

"Grandpa, do kids like me ever get shot by Cupid's arrow," I asked next.

"No!" he answered. "You've got a breathin' space before that happens. But jest you watch out when you get to be sixteen, or thereabouts," he cautioned.

I musta' sighed audibly with relief. This caught Grandpa's attention and he all but roared at me, "Heavenly days, boy, don't tell me that you think you're in love. At your age?" he added as he regarded me as he might a leper. "What you need is some good advice about wimmin, and by golly, you came to the right place to get it,' he said.

All of a sudden I felt trapped. The very thought of being in love made queasy sensations run up and down my spine. Why Grandpa misunderstood, I didn't know. Afraid to say more, I sat there as Grandpa entered upon a tirade against the fair sex that only made me wish he had a better opinion of them, waitin' for him to stop, which he finally did after gettin' back to Eve in the Garden of Eden.

"There, boy!" he snapped, as he finished. Take my advice and be wary of them critters. He was very pleased with himself, I could see. Revenge on "them critters" was an obsession with him. I decided the arrow of love had fallen out of his heart long ago. What he told me had no answers to my questions.

After thankin' Grandpa, I trundled on homeward, walkin' naturally, no longer fearin' Cupid's arrow, but still unsatisfied in my mind. What I really wanted to know was, I guess, what love really was. I loved my mother without bein' shot that I know'd of. I loved candy, which didn't seem to involve arrows at all. I loved gettin' even with Melvin without that supplyin' any help. What was this kind of love that grabbed everybody on February 14th, and caused that barebottomed bowman to fire his shafts at hearts, generating huggin' and kissin' like I saw the high school kids doin' at noon hour?

"Ma," I asked on arriving at home, "What is love?"

Ma seemed taken aback by this question, comin' as it did, out of the blue. She sat me down in a chair beside her, and behavin' like she would years later when she told me the secret of where I came from, soundin' like a teacher, said.

"Son, love is what makes the world go 'round. It's what caused me to marry your daddy. It's a feelin' so powerful that you can't resist it. That's what love is." Here she patted me on the head as if she were glad to have survived that ordeal.

"Ma," I said ---

"That's enough!" she said sharply before I could finish. "Go to bed, young man," And so I did, there to dream that Wilma hugged and kissed me until Josephine beat her up good and took over herself. I awakened next morning squirming to free myself from the badly tangled bed clothes.

Ah, Josephine, how like a no-holds-barred wrestling match you made it seem when you introduced me to the realm of romance. Had I come to consider love no more than the suffocating experience you made it seem, I might now be a confirmed bachelor. But I grew up and girls became interesting creatures; then one day, when I most should have been walkin' backwards, the little son-of-a-gun shot me, and that mush on the back of valentines was mush no longer. God Bless you, Josephine, whomever you're squeezin' now.

################################

A man's ego is his finest apparel; clad in it he struts, stripped of it he crumbles. How ironic that man's own rib most menaces his pride and self-esteem, having been fashioned into a woman.

(Notice: Equal space furnished for ego-puncturing comments.)

1988   THE OLD MAIDS Vs. PROGRESS

PREFACE

In our democracy, the Common Good is paramount, and all that is accomplished under its aegis takes precedence over individual rights. Few would disagree with the principle. It is fairly and justly upheld.

The Common Good and Progress appear to be almost identical in this regard. Anyway, the public must yield to the one and concede to the other.

Progress, in its irresistible excursions through time and place, requires sacrifice on the part of individuals in the interest of the Common Good. But, Progress is all too often a rude and brazen intruder upon the peace and security of the individual, whose recourse is no more than feeble at best. Opposition frequently develops to the methods of Progress, only to be beaten back or crushed ruthlessly by its relentless forward movement. In the instance related in the following pages, opposition to Progress takes on an absurd and comical aspect (or perhaps the sensitive reader will choose to regard it as pathetic) as useless as any other pose in resistance to the inevitable march of that swaggering giant, Progress.

First, you must join me in a journey back in time to the 1920's to a certain village of sleepy character in the great Mid-West; then straightway to the corner of West and Grove Streets where we find standing an old two-storied house of deteriorating appearance, which has been for many years the home of two old maids, sisters in fact. Both of these women are white-haired, wrinkled, shrill of voice, shabby of dress, sharp-featured and surpassingly disagreeable. They are reclusive in their habits, only infrequently spotted, though often heard by their neighbors as they move about inside their bush and vine entangled backyard, where they keep chickens in a tottering old coop and work a sizeable vegetable garden. In wintertime, they all but disappear from view. It is then that neighbors watch for curls of smoke from the chimney to be convinced that they still exist. Were they to store themselves in mothballs for winter's duration, they would be no more hidden from view.

The neighborhood surrounding these two old maids is one of modest, to less than modest, homes, peopled by families with limited incomes, struggling to keep ahead of debt. The men are either unskilled laborers or factory hands, away from home much of the day. Their womenfolk are, as a group, homemakers and childbearers, being more competent in the latter than the former, as a visit to their homes to count heads and check for tidiness will bear out. All of them, man, woman and child have, at one time or another, been in violent dispute with the two old maids; and not one of them has a good opinion to express. It is correct to say that these old maids have as many friends as they deserve--none.

This neighborhood is so overrun with youngsters that its streets ring with their shouts and laughter all day long, as they play, fight, and grow. The old maids and the children are constant antagonists. Teasing and tantalizing the two old women is one of their regular sports. This practice draws a fierce reaction from the old maids, as impertinence and disrespect should. Threats of harm to the children's physical welfare are common. Although, while the witch-like appearance of the threatening pair scares some, it encourages others. Mothers from nearby houses make it their practice to order the children away, when aware of these encounters, to practice their mischief elsewhere on persons only normally outraged by it.

So cantankerous and ill-humored are these two viragos, that when not embroiled in tangles with others, vent their spleen on each other. They are often heard arguing and wrangling between themselves, and neighbors joke about it, suggesting that they are practising their uncivil arts and honing up their sharp tongues. If witches were a reality, here was certainly a pair of them.

The injustice of mockery and scorn, as a means of expressing dislike or contempt, will be admitted, even by those who indulge in them, if called to account. The practice is especially prevalent in childhood, where the struggle for recognition and status assumes a magnified importance. We have all been its victims, and all known its humiliation. In fact, we have all made use of it at one time or another. It is a practice that appears to be rooted in the false belief that one can build himself up by beating others down.

This was the way it was in the 1920's, in that certain village on the corner of West and Grove Streets; but, lurking in the wings and eager to descend on the area was that rude invader, Progress. If progress were to invade here, toes were to be stepped upon, sensitive toes that once bruised would kick back with a vengeance.

The 1920's were a period of startling change, and progress was running rampant upon the scene, and in a dozen different directions at once. Those abreast of the times knew that inventors (ignoring the fact that history was already a confusion of names) had only lately as time goes, created the motor car, the electric light, the telephone and the radio. Others who didn't know, or didn't care, or couldn't afford these items anyway, seemed just as happy in ignorance of it. It was a dead certainty that the old maids had no patience with any new-fangled inventions, and could be relied on as staunch guardians of the old and the established.

The immensity of its task made progress slow to delve into those recesses where the demand for it was slow to generate, and financial reconsiderations made it seem unprofitable besides. The area of our consideration was one such recess, hardly eager for progress, but near to receiving it anyway.

It was early one summer morning that progress intruded upon West Street's isolation, to stick in its invasive nose, come prepared to bring its advantages to this street's inhabitants, whether wanted or not. Appearing in that guise, and hardly looking to be the heralds of the new, came a work crew of four men with the latest in equipment and machinery in tow. They bore the unmistakeable evidence of being company workmen; a decided lack of haste, a fumbling way of going at it, and a premonitory instinct for quitting time.

Once underway they progressed along West Street, a not very long thoroughfare, with deliberate speed; and when the noon hour came, lounged on the grassy roadbank, opened their lunch pails, and proceeded with still more deliberate speed to stretch an hour into unrecognizable shape. Back at it once again, they soon had placed light poles up to the corner of

West and Grove Streets. It then came about that the very next pole was to be erected beside that long established sanctuary for everything that was opposed to progress, in whatever form or shape--the Old Maids' home.

Machinery was brought to the spot, and drilling of the posthole began. In no time it was completed and the machinery removed. It was exactly at that moment that there blew out of that decaying house two bundles of animated rags, as if propelled by steam pressure emitting the most dreadful shrieks, while assaulting the air with a violent wind-milling of arms, bent on driving away those officious meddlers, and stalling progress in its tracks - the old maids.

Stunned by the suddenness of it, intimidated by the threat in it, and momentarily too confused by it to comprehend what was happening; then, recovering their senses instantly, the men made for the roadway with alacrity. Their hasty retreat encouraged the pair of termagants to increase their din, and brought to the sidelines a sizeable number of curious and amused spectators from nearby residences. Their appearance seemed to spur on the protesting, as the home crowd is known to inspire a sports team. They danced about like dervishes, swung their arms about with new enthusiasm, and added a series of discursive expletives to their rantings. All at once, as if inspired, they began to circle the posthole like witches around a caldron, while the appreciative and growing audience became hysterical in their laughter, and started shouting encouragement to the performers, and applauding mightily.

Not to omit entirely the second part of the cast, the onlookers, for no reason, turned to hooting and jeering the workmen for their pusillanimous reaction, as they stood in the roadway looking stupidly at each other, confounded as to what to do. Out of this fog of indecision, as if prodded to action by the abuse of the crowd, the boss of the work crew all at once becoming aware of the responsibilities of his position, left the group and began walking toward the two old hags, possibly with the intention of parleying, perhaps to assure them that nothing was to be done that would in any way be upsetting to two such nice old ladies as themselves.

He got about halfway to his target when the two "nice old ladies" made him a target for sticks, stones, pieces of broken glass, anything about and available. Dodging debris, with his arms held before his face for protection, he was back with his crew members in jig time, suffering more humiliation in the face of loud and uncontrollable laughter and deprecatory comments, boisterously delivered from an audience simply overcome with delight, and near to being doubled over from pure enjoyment.

Thereupon the boss held a brief conference with his men and another decision was reached, and quickly. What was decided became known when all four, sheep-like, began to march to their parked vehicle which they entered and drove off amid catcalls and hoots of derision from a disappointed audience, whose actors, part of them anyway, had left the stage before the drama was ended to their satisfaction.

Voicing disappointment with mutterings and grumbles, but still able and willing to chuckle in gleeful fashion as they recalled the previous actions of the old maids, and the response of the workmen, as if assuming that the fun was ended. At least for the time being, the onlookers began to head back to a resumption of their daily routine. The old maids, on the contrary, took the opportunity to hurl at the departing spectators a few shrill and biting comments, not at all laudatory, and some even profane in character.

Now that they were, more or less, left to themselves, with the exception of a few neighbor women who took stations behind curtained windows of their homes prepared to alert all interested should anything new develop, these two warriors of the forces of opposition, sensing correctly that the present lull would not last, got busy at consolidating their gains and strengthening their defenses, as if schooled in military tactics. Cackling away like chickens after a disturbance in the coop, they set about renewing their supply of rubble, stones--handy for throwing, sticks--just the thing for clubbing, and a pail of washwater--very appropriate as a chaser. These details accomplished, they resumed their normal relationship, that of carping at one another over trifles.

Surely, as a result of the excitement undergone earlier, the pair, surly and quarrelsome, suddenly interrupted a venting of malice on each other and began walking around the posthole, eyeing it with disapproval, while seeming at the same time to be in discussion, and trying to reach a decision agreeable to both. Abruptly, they ceased parading. Immediately the older of the two sat down on the grass beside the hole, gathered her long dark skirts in her arms, and, with a flurry of yardgoods and the revelation of endless quantities of dingy fabric, uncovered a pair of spindly legs clad in black stockings, much darned and patched, swung them awkwardly over the hole and directed them into it. Following this, she inched herself forward, and by wriggling and squirming, let follow as much of herself as the hole would accommodate. Aided by her sister, in a querulous manner, the two spread out her voluminous skirts in a circle about her, covering her lower self and the hole completely. After this maneuver, the younger sister took a position at her side with a club in hand and resting on her shoulder, looking much like a sentry on duty. Both were now positioned for whatever was to ensue.

Just look at her; half in and half out of a hole in the ground. She must be well into her sixties, if not older. Notice the discomfort she suffers. How ridiculous!

Time went by; ten minutes, twenty minutes, twenty-five minutes, and the Old One began to tire. The scouts sitting at windows began to tire of just looking on. The Old One became peevish and complaining. Where was Progress? It couldn't be successfully thwarted and surrendering, could it? No, of course not. But where was it? What was holding it up?

It came time for a changing of the guard. The Old One had proven her sturdiness and hardihood beyond doubting, and under circumstances seldom duplicated in day-to-day living. It was a feat to be admired in a woman of her advanced years.

Before the change could be made, the Old One had to be extricated from her imprisonment in the posthole; and that was to be difficult to manage. The Younger One squatted down, took hold of her sister by the underarms, and with an exhausting effort on the parts of both, managed to free her. Too spent then to do otherwise, both sat on the grass gasping for breath. When able, they struggled to their feet, and the younger sister prepared to descend into the hole.

It happened that this sister was a good foot shorter than the other, more rotund, and considerably wider in the hips, all of which predicted difficulty. She sat down, found her legs in less ungainly fashion than had the other, and dropped them into the hole for a start. Next, she inched forward as her sister had done and began the descent. At hip level she became stuck, and with a struggle pulled herself back out again. Using sticks, both women worked to enlarge the hole at the mouth. Again she made the attempt to descend. With a screwing motion of her body, she succeeded, sinking to her armpits in the ground, ending up with clothing badly rumpled, short of breath, and with heavy head of hair looking like an inverted chicken nest, as its pinned-up former state was loosened from her extraordinary effort. It was readily apparent that getting her out, when the time came, was to be a Herculean task.

All this was hardly accomplished when, as if to pile indignity upon indignity, as though being beset by the emissaries of progress wasn't enough, the elements now chose to add their harassment to all that had been previously endured by the tormented old maids. It began to rain, softly at first; then in a downpour. The Old One ran to the house--that is to say, she made for the house with all the speed she could muster--to return quickly with an umbrella that displayed such a state of degeneration as to appear, when opened, to have more use as a water-catcher than a water-shedder. She moved close to her half-buried sister, held this useless article over both their heads to very little purpose, as you may imagine; and both suffered a drenching, especially the younger one, as water from the umbrella ran into the hole to saturate her feet.

Thankfully, the rain was soon over. Spectators had fled to nearby porches, too interested in what was happening to wish to miss any of it. After the rain, the sun came out hot on the bedraggled pair at the posthole, causing a vapor to rise from their sodden clothing. Now the sorry pair looked like two scarecrows in a morning fog. But there was no indication from either that they had lost any of their stubborn determination to persist in this inane resistance to the inevitable.

Almost as if mercy had a thought for their plight, a company vehicle drove up and parked nearby.

Out of this vehicle emerged three men, one of whom was quickly recognized as the crew boss, involved so discreditably in the earlier episode. The second out was a person of commanding appearance, tall, heavy, greyish about the temples, and dressed in suit and tie. He was promptly judged by the knowing women in the gathered assemblage to be a "higher-up" from company headquarters. Last out was a middle aged man, thickset, double-chinned, with good bearing, but wearing a most doleful expression on his homely face, as if he was perpetually in mourning. He moved at a set and lumbering pace, wore the badge of a constable and was well known in the village, only in his official capacity.

The trio consulted briefly, then began to walk slowly toward the entrenched and drenched troublemakers. This was the signal for the Old Maids to renew the ranting that had marked their earlier set-to with the boss and his crew. The expectations of the crowd heightened, and they moved nearer. With each forward pace by the three men, the Old Maids carried on louder and louder until they were once more screeching like mad women.

When within twenty yards of these hellcats, the crew boss and the constable stopped, and allowed the company official--if that was what he was--to proceed alone. He walked confidently forward, as if assured that he could handle the situation. When within a few yards of the old women, he began to reason with them in a calm voice saying that there had been a misunderstanding for which he apologized, that the difficulty could be resolved would they but listen to him. He got that much said when a gob of mud hit him full in the chest, and others following, while missing him, went by near enough to his person to spatter him in several places. The Old Maids were making good use of the dirt left from the drilling of the posthole, and turned to mud by the rain.

This greeting stopped him where he stood. With a complete change of attitude he now began to "lay down the law" to his assailants in a loud voice, trembling with anger and disgust. He announced the company's rights, and spelled out the legal penalties for anyone guilty of attempting to interfere. He was blunt, he was harsh, and he made it clear that tomfoolery was to be no longer tolerated. With this, he moved back to the company of the other two men, using a clean, white handkerchief to wipe mud from his clothing.

Nothing he had said had any effect at all on the Old Maids, who continued to scream away. It is doubtful if they heard what he said, for it may have been inaudible to them over their own din. The Old Maids persisted, and the spectators applauded enthusiastically.

Now it was the constable's turn to approach. He moved slowly and deliberately forward. He came nearer and nearer. Strangely, nothing was thrown. He came nearer still, and, as if a record played were turned off, both Old Maids ceased their bedlam of noise, dropped their weapons, and in an unbelievable change of demeanor, appeared docile and subdued.

"What goes on here?" This behavior is totally unexpected and completely alien to such bad-natured old women as the two old maids. It's inexplicable! It's anticlimactic! Do our eyes deceive us? No! What we actually saw actually happened. "What power has this constable over the old maids?" Such questions run through the gathered spectators, and without answers.

The constable, still wearing his sad-eyed look, and moving slowly, walked up to the Old One, and in the gentlest of tones, spoke to her. As she listened she began to hang her head as if ashamed. He next moved to the sister still implanted in the earth and bending down, grasped hold of her. Using all his considerable strength, he pulled her up and stood her on her feet. He talked briefly to her and evoked the same result. Submissively, each permitted him to take an arm in hand and lead both to the house, which they entered and disappeared as he stood watching them go.

Many strange things happen in the society of mankind. This event had to be listed as one of them. It was as if the onlookers had been watching a drama that ended when the players walked off the stage in the middle of Act II. Disappointment and amazement held all in a state of silent unbelief. As they stood thus, the constable moved to confront them, bade them return to their homes, assuring them that there was no longer any reason for staying. He remained to see his instructions obeyed, then walked to the company vehicle, and with the two men who came with him got in and all departed the scene.

Well! Well! Progress is again the victor. This time over two spunky old maids; next time, who knows who will be trampled upon. Progress being as bold and brazen, as insensitive, as implacable in intent, as resolute in purpose as it is, shouldn't all concede to its demands, and spare themselves the pain of being bulldozed into acceptance? It would seem so, but some, like the old maids, must be convinced, nevertheless.

Years went by, and the mystery went unsolved. If there was an explanation, and there had to be, it was hidden beyond uncovering. Electric lights began to gleam in homes along West Street; telephone lines, newly installed, hummed with messages; radios blared music and news from many points and automobiles raced along its length; but there were no such changes at the old maids' domicile. They did, however, have an intruder, one less welcome than Progress--death. It came to still the heart of the Old One and bring an end to her stormy and rigorous existence.

News of her death revived gossip that had all but died out beforehand, and drew from retirement speculation concerning the mysterious power held by the constable over the old maids. But, all was still in vain. The mystery remained a mystery.

A funeral followed, of course. Apart from those present in some official capacity, two who could be considered mourners were in attendance, the Young One and the Constable. Which of the two felt the loss most deeply was hard to judge. The sister wailed and carried on in a manner little short of disgusting. The constable seemed genuinely distressed, and the tear that wet his coarse cheek was unquestionably shed in honest grief.

Reports of the behavior of those two finding their way to West Street, the buzzing that went on there picked up in volume. When, later in the week, it leaked out that the expense of the burial had come from the constable's pocket, it rose still more. The bones of past events, having been picked clean, new and fleshy ones were needed for this malicious crew, and they kept coming. It was an extended feast for them.

When it was noticed and reported that the Old One's sister did not return to the house on the corner after the funeral, it was like being served up a new course during a meal. No one knew why she didn't return, or where she had gone. All that could be offered in the way of explanation was an eyewitness revelation that, following the funeral, she had left in a car driven by the constable, heading east. What a delicious morsel this was. It permitted unlimited speculation, and got it. The tongue-waggers of West Street now placed her safely with relatives; again, in the county insane asylum; and, ultimately, in some desolate roadside spot, the victim of a cruel murderer. It seemed the less known, the more preposterous the speculations became.

Two weeks had passed without news when the constable appeared at the house, entered with a key, drew down the tattered shades on the windows, closed and locked all doors, and, before leaving, erected a "For Sale" sign on the skimpy front lawn--actually bare dirt. To some this seemed confirmation that the Young One was truly dead.

The mystery of it was teasing, and one competed with another in concocting explanations, none very satisfying. The frustration this caused for one already suffering from acute nervousness was enough to send her to the local doctor's office for relief. The old doctor, being a shrewd one, knew his patients inside out. After prescribing and supplying some pills, he expressed the professional opinion that the patient's distress was likely due to the hot weather and the onset of menopause. The pills were to soothe her nerves and the opinion was to buck up her spirits. The thought that her childbearing days were limited was so pleasing to this one, that she returned home delighted and fully recovered.

With the closing of the house, nothing at all happened to inject new life into the gossip on West Street. Winter came, dark windows and a smokeless chimney provided only memories of hectic times of the past. For lack of sustenance, rumor and speculation turned elsewhere.

Spring came, houses were opened up to its pleasant breezes, early flowers bloomed, and leaves began to green the caps of trees. The sexton of the village cemetery on the edge of town, an elderly gentleman, felt the stirrings of the season in his heart and aching limbs. It was like a tonic, and he wore an incipient smile on his face, detectable only at the corners of the mouth, but still an improvement, nevertheless, over his usual stoic facade. The growing population indebted to him for care and attention, being a moulding and mute lot, weren't likely to demonstrate or express appreciation for anything done on their behalf, or care one way or the other what look he wore on his face. Springtime was a busy time for the sexton. Raking leaves, collecting winter's refuse, a little sodding here, a shovel full of dirt there, a marker straightened yonder; he had much to do, and he went at it whistling in competition with the newly arrived birds.

He was busily engaged when a flat-bed truck drove through the iron gateway of the cemetery and pulled to a stop. It was annoying to have interruptions of his work, and he showed resentment. He stood leaning on the rake handle, resting his chin on his hands, and staring belligerently at the intruding vehicle, showing no intention of moving. Out of the truck cab came a man garbed in grey coveralls. He approached the sexton with the attitude of one in search of information, asked for and got directions to a certain gravesite, returned to the truck and moved it to the desired plot. Two men emerged this time, uncovered a headstone on its rear platform, together lifted it and set it on the platform's edge, jumped to the ground, picked it up again and staggered with it to a grassless spot, barren from a previous burial. Carefully they set it in place, returned to the truck, got in and drove away.

The sexton knew from memory whose grave it was, but as the caretaker he felt the need to become immediately familiar with all changes in his domain. He laid down his rake and walked to the site where he stood a while looking over the changed appearance. He remarked to himself: "It ain't much of a stone. Good enough, I guess, for her." He read its inscription critically and commented once again: "They must have that wrong. Probably belongs to someone else," turned about and returned to his work.

Back at his residence, which happened to be on Grove Street, not far from the corner of West Street, his daily stint as sexton over, he casually mentioned to his wife at supper that the old maid who died last fall finally got a headstone for her grave. This good woman was a prominent member of the gossiping sorority, and was quick to recognize that she now had a hold on an item that, when divulged to her sisters of the West Street Clacking Club, would make her the center of attention and win her their undivided admiration. She saw to it that she got every detail her husband could provide, left her meal half-eaten, and went promptly to the telephone.

Say what you will, this remarkable invention, lately installed, provides the best possible means of spreading gossip with dispatch. She rang, lifted the receiver, and was greeted by the voice of Central requesting, "Number please." All praise given, still one had to acknowledge that even an amazing invention like the telephone has its shortcomings. Central had an ear for gossip, and had been known to use the advantages of the switchboard to outrace callers, and disseminate choice bits of news before the party calling could complete her rounds. It was an unavoidable hazard.

"I can't believe it!" was the common response on the other end of the line. "Are you sure?" was incredulously asked. It was the teasingest tidbit to develop out of the whole affair. She let it out like a fisherman does his hand-line, a few inches at a time, procrastinating as long as she could, and dropping the bombshell for a climax. It was such great fun, she thought. After completing her calls, after savoring the pleasure from the stir she caused, she sat down again at the table and made the same remark herself, "I can't believe it!"

Believed or not, the headstone was there as verification, and for all to see, if they chose. And what was on the headstone over the Old One's barren gravesite? It was the simplest of inscriptions: just one word, "Mother."

Of all the wild speculations dredged up out of contorted minds, this was one possibility completely overlooked on West Street. Shock and amazement, the first reactions, were followed by a doubting attitude before acceptance. "Mother! Who's mother? But she wasn't married! I never saw her with a man-- except the constable, that is. The constable! You don't suppose?--

So it went its course throughout West Street, and much beyond. The constable was accepted as the likeliest target for suspicion. That he was the father of the Old One's unknown illegitimate child was, more or less, agreed upon; and it was stated more than once that he should be forced to resign for the honor and good name of the village; but always privately, never openly.

Many months passed. The constable, unaware that he had been the victim of calumny, performed his duties as usual.

Then, one dark night he happened upon a burglary in progress at the General Store. Bravely he attempted to apprehend the criminals, but was severely wounded in the attempt. Rushed to a hospital in a nearby city, he died within a few hours.

Again there was a funeral, only this one was largely attended. "He was a brave man," said one resident of West Street, "and he deserves to be paid respect." All agreed. So he was eulogized by prominent citizens. Then he was laid to rest. Where? Beside the Old One, and his headstone, when placed, was as simple in its message as hers. With one word it solved the persistent mystery without alleviating one iota of the gossip and what could be sweeter to the West Street Clackers. The marker bore the inscription "Son".

################################

I had been fishing all day. I was tired and hungry. Everything with an edible aspect tempted me as I came upon it, berries on bushes, succulent-appearing plants. I became ravenous, but sanity restrained me. This experience made me wonder about our early ancestors. Who decided what to eat, and what not to eat? It has to be that some hungry forbear of ours dared the temptation to become the pioneer of food-tasters. If he ate it and lived, it was added to the human diet, and if it wasn't and he didn't---? Oh, well! Since we are here, our ancestors had to have been judicious, and left the sampling to others. Let us offer thanks for their timidity and discretion as we mourn those who discovered the poisonous and the indigestible at a heavy price.

1979   HIGH LOVE: A ROMANCE IN FOUR EPISODES

HIGH LOVE EPISODE I

He was a stranger in town, a lean, lanky, handsome youth who stood six feet, six inches in height. He was of marriageable age, and suffering from the silly belief that he could choose whomever he wished to be his future bride. This to be done in the same fashion as he would use in selecting a car that pleased his fancy. He was now on a scouting trip for that purpose. He had earlier decided on the sort of girl he wanted, and failing to find her among the eligible prospects in his home town, was now widening his search: This accounts for his presence this day in the neighboring village.

What were the criteria he had established? Rather exacting ones, I'd say. She must be pretty, shapely, of fair complexion, virtuous, intelligent, sensible, charming, delicate, and above all, near his own height. That she existed, he had no doubt. "Where?" was now the question. Thus his presence as a stranger in another town.

"Will he find this epitome of girlhood? Watch for next week's episode.

HIGH LOVE EPISODE II

You will recall that our six foot, six inch stranger was in town seeking his soul-mate. Where better could he post himself for this purpose than on Main Street, where passing samples of femininity would be most prevalent this summer day? To best meld into the scenery and escape notice, he stood close to a telephone pole, which, with its similar lineaments, made him all but invisible to the train of passing humanity. Referring now and then to his nine point criteria, he gauged each prospect as she passed by, and had dismissed all as unsuitable, when the noon hour approached, and hunger's call aroused his considerable appetite for food. It was then that he broke off his vigil, left the telephone pole to support itself, and ambled toward a cafe sign he had spotted.

On entering this place of business his eyes alighted upon its sole visible occupant, the waitress, so identified by the uniform she wore. The mere sight of her stopped our youth dead in his tracks and put his eyeballs in danger of everting in their sockets.

Is love's call answered? Watch for next week's episode!

HIGH LOVE EPISODE III

The cafe our tall stranger entered had the usual square tables, covered with red and white checkered cloths, matching the puckered curtains over its windows. On his right ran a long counter, and it was behind this fixture that this vision of loveliness stood, without difficulty reaching up to replace a burned-out light bulb. Mentally, in a split second, he raced through his nine criteria for a wife, making comparison with what he beheld; and was happily--somewhat amazingly--able to verify each, including the most crucial one, height. She fit the mold perfectly, or the mold fit her perfectly, however you would regard it.

The heat of his elation unfroze him from his stalled stance, and he moved to the counter, engaged her sparkling eyes on a level plane, and silently poured into those portals of the soul all that in love's compendium goes unspoken. She, in return, instantly struck by Cupid's arrow, responded with equal ardor and with identical sentiment in the same silent, but none-the-less convincing lexicon of love.

Has the search ended? Don't miss next week's final episode.

HIGH LOVE EPISODE IV

We left our pair in eyeball to eyeball expositions of unspoken love. To continue:

As discreet persons we should avert our gaze--but we won't, will you?

There they stood, instantly enamoured of each other, unaware of all else, until she, suddenly awakened to indiscretion, dropped her lily-white hands to the counter and, in sprightly fashion, dismounted from the stool on which she had been standing. From her new position on the floor, and from her new elevation of five feet, she looked up-slope into his eyes; and, in her capacity as waitress, requested to know his desire, as if she hadn't already read it in his eyes.

At this point, we can well imagine the turmoil going on in this young man's mind. There she stood, flagrantly in violation of criterion IX, one and one-half feet of bitter disappointment, sprung upon him so suddenly as to create the most devastating confusion he had ever faced in his young life. Broken, for an instant, was his delectable contact with love's heaven.

Well, maybe you can understand by what contorted reasoning he resolved the issue when to himself he said: "Eight out of nine ain't bad! I'll buy her a stool for a wedding present!" ---and so he did.

########## LABOR TROUBLE ##########

While I acknowledge the justice of the complaint by Doc Maycroft that he received a blank copy of the bulletin, I fear that there is little understanding of the circumstances involved. Ordinarily I would have fired the staff member responsible for this faux pas, but the consequences of such an action stared me in the face. You see, had I fired her I would have lost my typist, my printer, my stamper, my mailer, and my meals. So I took the only step I could; I called in the entire staff, and in my most severe manner said, "Dear, next time I write a blank bulletin would you please bring it home and bawl me out?"

########## PREJUDICE ##########

"A rose, is a rose, is a rose," but the dandelion is a weed, is a weed, is a weed -- or is it? Why must this lovely little golden button of a bloom, without thorns, formed like nothing else to fit in a buttonhole, be so degraded? He who made that unfair distinction was a clod not a poet. Roses fade and die while the dandelion lasts and lasts, despite all irrational attempts to annihilate it; and can, and will, most obligingly, make a flower-bed of an entire lawn without effort or expense. I, for one, am pro-dandelion. Why, it grieves me no end to decapitate them with a mower to uncover the drab green grass.

PRO AND CON 1968

Some people are known for what they are "for"; others are known for what they are "against." I observe that those who are for something speak out when the opportunity presents itself, while those who are against things are more zealous, and go about creating situations which give them a chance to express their opposition. I also observe that the "againers" are inclined to be intolerant of other people's views, and to associate themselves together to strengthen their opinions.

To understand what I mean, take the dandelion, for instance: some people are for it, and some are against it. At this time of year when dandelions are so abundant, and are dotting lawns like so many little yellow buttons, the "againers" are running to the store for weedkiller to murder them in cold chemicals.

Now I ask you, what's really wrong with a few billion dandelions that they should be exterminated: Do they harm people? No! Of course, they don't! You kick this thought around a little bit and you must come to the conclusion that some people prefer the green color of the grass to the yellow color of the dandelion. And you further conclude that if dandelions were green and grass were yellow, that people would rush to the store to buy fertilizer for dandelions and grasskiller for the grass.

Or you could come to the conclusion that some people like the sword-shape of a blade of grass, and dislike the shield shape of the dandelion, and you decide that such people are aggressive people who like to kill things. It is very doubtful if these anti-dandelion people have ever picked a dandelion and examined the flower carefully. It is a thing of beauty, really, delicately fashioned of many tiny petals shaped in a wheel of golden loveliness that should impress any and all.

Of course, the dandelion has no aroma to please the sense of smell, and when pressed to the nose stains it with a butter color. So what? Look at them, don't smell them. When left on the lawn, they age and become balls of grey lace from which seeds drift onto the neighbor's lawn, and the following year he has more beautiful dandelions than you do. But far from appreciating this fact, your neighbor, who is probably anti-dandelion, gets nasty, and suggests that you should kill your dandelions so that he can keep them off his lawn, which makes you mad because your neighbor has a dog which he lets run free, and who digs holes in your lawn. So you say to your neighbor, "My dandelions bother you, but your dog bothers me," and your neighbor says to you, "How can you compare a living creature like a dog to a weed?" And you say to your neighbor: "My dandelions are alive, aren't they?" And your neighbor gets so angry that he won't speak to you, so you build a fence between your homes to keep his dog off your lawn, and when you are on vacation he comes over and sprays your lawn with weedkiller and executes your lovely dandelions.

Now if people weren't against so many things this wouldn't have happened. Your neighbor's dog would still be digging holes in your lawn, and your dandelions would still be seeding his lawn, and the two of you would still be getting along unhappily.

Well, after your neighbor has killed your dandelions, he feels ashamed of himself because your dandelions are dead, but his dog is alive; so he ties up his dog on a chain, and the dog howls and howls until you feel that you are going out of your mind, and you think about loading your gun and shooting the noisy beast, but your wife restrains you, and she speaks to the neighbor's wife about the howling of the dog, and the neighbor's wife says something back about your kids, and they won't speak to each other after that, and the dog keeps on howling so you walk around the yard wearing ear-muffs so that the whole neighborhood will understand your feelings. And your neighbor retaliates by refusing to buy garden seeds which your kids are selling, and ordering them off his property. Then your kids get into fights with their kids, and they won't play together any longer.

So here you are with hostile neighbors and no beautiful dandelions on your lawn. After a time you come to accept this fact, and you suffer from remorse because of your childish actions; so you take down the fence which is bent anyway where your neighbor's wife hit it with the car, and you say to yourself: "Life is too short to waste it with this kind of foolishness." You are even happy when the neighbor lets his dog loose from the chain and he comes back to dig holes in your lawn.

Then one spring day you notice that some dandelions are growing on your nice green lawn, with holes in it, so you rush down to the store for some weedkiller, and promptly execute them, while your neighbor notices that some dandelions are growing on his lawn which he lets grow because he has wearied of the fight which is evidence that he has abandoned his anti-dandelion attitude at the same time that you have become anti-dandelion.

Now where are you? If you only had a dog that dug holes in your neighbor's lawn, you would, in all practicality, have reversed your roles, and who knows that you wouldn't be more anti-dandelion than your neighbor ever was?

All this trouble over dandelions could have been avoided, of course, had these two families practised the golden rule, had they done to others as they would have others do to them. If the man who had the dandelions in the first place had used weedkiller on them, and killed them so that the fuzzy seeds would not have blown onto his neighbor's lawn, or if the neighbor who used the weedkiller on his lawn had not used it, then the dandelions would have grown on his lawn and the fuzzy little seeds would have blown onto your lawn. And if the neighbor with the dog had tied him up in the first place so he could howl, but not dig holes in your lawn, then the wives and kids could have been mad at each other without the dandelions figuring in the controversy.

Now, if your wife is mad at the neighbor's wife, and your kids are fighting with the neighbor's kids, whether you are pro-dandelion or anti-dandelion doesn't really matter, nor does it matter which way the fuzzy little dandelion seeds are blowing, nor does it matter who owns the dog that digs the holes in the lawn, or is tied up and howling, because you already have enough cause to hate your neighbor.

But everyone knows that you are supposed to love your neighbor, so you think of some way to express to him your wish to get along. Since you now have no dandelions on your lawn, you walk over on his lawn and pick a bouquet of these little yellow troublemakers, knock on his door, and when he appears, you hand them to him as a peace offering. He is overcome by this gesture of friendship on your part, and becomes so emotional that he is near tears, and without thinking buries his face in the lovely bouquet of dandelions which you have picked from his lawn and given him, and when he withdraws his face from the blossoms it is so covered with yellow that he looks like a chinaman, and you break out laughing, and he, thinking that you are just happy about the reconciliation, laughs too. From somewhere inside the house his wife appears because she wonders what is going on, and when she sees her husband's yellow face, she begins to laugh, and this makes him mad because he doesn't like to have his wife embarrass him in front of other people, so he takes his lovely bouquet of dandelions, given him as a peace offering, and rams them into her laughing face.

Well, these two men who lived side by side were once again on friendly terms, but from that time on the neighbor and his wife didn't get along well together. In a short time she left her husband, got a divorce, their kids became delinquents, the husband began to drink heavily, and lost his job. He finally squandered all his money, and lost his home because he failed to keep up his payments on the mortgage.

Now the moral of the story is: Don't laugh until you get yellow in the face.

################################

The old values are being knocked apart by our captious youth. It is as if the Rock of Ages had begun to crumble and splinter. Once, I recall vividly, I knew right from wrong, good from bad, progress from retrogression, onward from backward, virtue from sin, white from black, and each day, as old values are assaulted, I become more and more confused and perplexed. This beleaguering of our time-honored bastions of stability, this rending of the abutments of morality, this belaboring of the capitalistic system, this wholesale attack upon government, education and religion; all this upsets my footing and leaves me teetering precariously as if an earthquake had shaken apart the world I knew and I had lost my bearings in the rubble.

You look poised and serene amidst it all. The more reason for me to admire you.

IMPERFECT
VIEW
VIGNETTES

1

It was Thursday evening, and some sort of women's gathering was going on in the living room. This relegated me to the kitchen where, with nothing else to do, I was wondering, for the hundredth time, why it was that the Pompeians had built their city near the foot of Mt. Vesuvius where, it and they were buried in lava in 79 B.C. Wandering on in thought, I asked myself this time why the Trojans had shown so little prudence by pulling a wooden horse inside their city walls before inspecting it with more care than they had shown; and why the citizens of Hamlin had refused to pay the piper after he had rid their city of rats, and had thereby lost their children.

I'm sure that I could have drifted on in this vein of thought through countless such events which defied explanation, but I was interrupted at this point by a woman who raised her ungentle voice in the declaration that all in the house were intended to hear. "Women should stand up and assert their rights!" she shouted, and this broke my train of thought momentarily.

After this Women's Liberationist had quieted down, and the buzz in the living room indicated that ways to bring about the liberation of women were under discussion and since I was confident that this would not happen before morning, I began to drift back to my previous thoughts, only to find that now, the idea of "rights" had intruded itself into my mind, and in the confusion of thoughts that I now engaged in, came the inspiration that these seemingly incongruous matters were related. In fact, I decided, the cases of the Pompeians, the Trojans and the Hamlinites were all splendid examples of the exercise of the less obvious of Man's--and for the benefit of the Women Liberationists in the living room--women's inalienable rights.

The Right that I am alluding to, I quickly realized, has no limitations upon its use, nor any choice in its possession. It could be said to be the plaything of the fool, an embarrassment to the wise, humiliation to the proud, defeat for the courageous, and profit to insurance companies who point to those who have used this right as a clinching argument in selling their policies.

Come to think of it, no right that Man possesses is more

inalienable than this particular one. No tyrant has ever been able to deny the use of it to his subjects, nor separate them from the possession of it even by the cruellest of tortures. No recluse has ever been able to seclude himself from it in any fastness on Earth; nor has any mother been able to spare her child the pain of it. The truth is that it is ours to exercise whether or not we desire.

It is not strange that this right is not enumerated in our Bill of Rights even though politicians are professionals in its use.

I have no doubt that you are using this right periodically. Was it you who said that the gun was not loaded? Or, are you the one who said: "That ice is thick enough to support my weight!" No? Then it must be you who said: "I can beat that train to the crossing."

I could get you sooner or later! Anyway, won't you agree with me that the ultimate use of this right was God's creation of Man?

"What right?" you ask. Why, the "Right to be Wrong", of course.

2

"Gentlemen, this is the Christmas Season, and the voters I represent--ably, I might add--expect Main Street to be decorated festively with tinsel and lights." It was Councilman Fairly expressing his views at a regular meeting of the Village Council and with his usual pomposity.

"Let me remind the councilman that funds are short, and this catering to the whims of the voters is subservient to our obligations of office. We were elected to the Council to exercise our good judgment, not to submit to public clamor." It was Council President Porcine speaking this time, and setting the stage for a genuine council argument, for this Village Council was badly rent with disagreement on all subjects other than a motion to increase their salaries.

"I suggest," continued President Porcine, "that rather than waste the town's funds, we offer a modest prize to that citizen who performs the most noble deed during the Yuletide."

Faced with these two proposals, the Village Council voted 4 to 3 for the latter, the split in its ranks favoring President Porcine.

Yuletide came and Councilman Porcine's committee, appointed by himself, chaired by himself, was alert for noble deeds with its eyes focused attentively upon the influential citizens in the town, and quite blind to what occurred elsewhere.

On Christmas eve the Council convened to render its decision and award the prize a fifty dollar savings bond. "I nominate--that is, my committee nominates--Henry Proud," said President Porcine, "his home decorations were outstanding and a credit to the whole community," and indeed, his beautifully lighted home, high on a hill, shed its colored beams on the whole community.

"My constituents nominate Sy Downer," said Councilman Fairly.

"That worthless bum!" shouted President Porcine to the amusement of his faithful four. "The only noble gesture he could possibly make would be to leave this community. Ha, Ha, Ha!"

"But he entered a burning home and saved the lives of two poor children, what could be nobler?" asked the affronted Councilman Fairly. "And he is now in the hospital seriously burned."

"Gentlemen," said Councilman Porcine, "you are wise in your decisions, I have nominated--my committee has nominated--Henry Proud for this honor. He is an outstanding, citizen, he operates the leading business in this town, and has contributed much to the town's growth and progress. Councilman Fairly (chuckle) has nominated Sy Downer whose reputation is likewise <u>well known</u> to you. We will vote!"

Of course, Henry Proud was voted winner 4 to 3. The prize was presented to him on Christmas Day with appropriate ceremony; and at about the same hour that Sy Downer passed away, a victim of his burns.

"This proves my point," said Councilman Porcine to his wife, as if to vindicate his judgment, "had I not forced the issue, Fairly's bunch would have awarded the prize to a dead man. This ought to assure me of re-election."

3

Abner was crazy, but Abner didn't realize that he was crazy. This attitude made it impossible to convince Abner that he was crazy, while it put Abner in a fine position to attack the sanity of the sane. With the most illogical logic Abner proceeded to do just that. Impervious as he was to reason or common sense, he argued that all others were mad, and with such self-assurance that his sane acquaintances began to doubt their sanity, and to endeavor to counter Abner's irrational arguments with irrational arguments of their own. Soon enough this caused one sane man to eye another sane man with suspicion and doubt, and to argue between themselves, while Abner heckled both with devilish glee, sensing cunningly that he was getting the upper hand.

When finally the situation became so bizarre and unreal that crazy Abner appeared less insane than the shouting frenzied men about him, there was no longer any doubt that Abner was victor over the situation, and temporary insanity had gripped the group of sane and reasonable men who had set out to convince Abner that he was crazy.

This raises the question whether being crazy and believing yourself sane is not a happier state of affairs than being sane and doubting it, and since I only fit into one category while you fit into the other, we must resolve the question jointly.

4

He walked through the woods and observed the struggle for life that went on there with silent and fierce intensity. He was struck by the seemingly meaningless tangle of plants that fought each other for living space, weakening themselves in their haste to outgrow their neighbors. He looked at the trees, and saw how they struggled upward, pushing their crowns toward the life-giving sunlight along slender trunks, and how they bent and twisted in the search. He stopped to examine two trees which grew side by side, and whose trunks were embraced in an inseparable wrestler's hold while their branches interlaced above. He saw the dead saplings that had lost in the struggle, and he became aware of the giants who had won their fight, and whose trunks grew fat with success as they spread their branches over an area where they held sway like emperors smothering all vegetation beneath.

"Ah, success in the struggle for survival," he thought, and then his awakened eye caught the parade of insects that probed the mighty tree trunk searching for a weak spot where they might sate their hunger and topple an empire.

Then the birds came to his attention as they fed on these same insects while pausing occasionally to peck among their feathers where parasites lived comfortably.

He heard the buzzing of flies which swarmed around the remains of an animal partly eaten by its enemy, and heard the splash as a fish in the nearby stream rose to the surface for a worm which had fallen there.

Suddenly the full reality of the struggle for survival dawned upon him and he became aware of the fragile protections that separated human beings from this struggle. "Thank God," he said aloud, "for intelligence and reason."

The fact that he was killed in an automobile accident on his way home was entirely unrelated to the struggle for existence. It was an accident; there was no premeditation, no intent to suicide, no survival of the fittest. It was all outside the scheme of things--or was it?

1980   5 TRUE LOVE

Amarilla was a loving and dutiful wife to Horace. Horace, for his part, was an appreciative and affectionate husband to Amarilla. Theirs was a blissful union.

How sad that Horace took ill. How sadder yet that Horace's condition worsened; and how utterly devastating that Horace passed away on the day before Christmas. Poor Amarilla was crushed and beside herself in grief.

Amarilla's grief, you see, was doubled by the fact that Horace had died of pneumonia, acquired as the result of a terrible cold he had contracted while working in wintry weather, inadequately clothed. There had been no money to meet the need. A sense of guilt, not rightly assumed, pricked her saddened heart.

"Why! Oh, why!" she wailed, "did you have to leave me?" "And why! oh, why! just before Christmas?"

Beneath the Christmas tree lay an unopened present from Amarilla to Horace. She had worked hard and long cleaning and sewing for neighbors and purchased this present with her earnings. It was a present to answer his need; come too late. Tears fell as Amarilla bemoaned her loss, and considered how death had robbed her of the eagerly anticipated joy of beholding the look of pleasure that was sure to enwreath Horace's face when he untied the package to reveal her gift of love.

In consideration for Amarilla's tender feelings--by special arrangement with the undertaker--much to Amarilla's comfort, Horace was buried in his brand-new, store-bought, red flannel underwear.

6

She didn't take well to criticism, this wife of his. (For that matter, what wife does?) Though himself not a perfectionist, he did appreciate a well-kept house. His immediate problem pertained to the familiar household chore of dusting, an increasing layer of which was deepening on window sills and furniture, attesting to her blindness to that need.

Because he held her good humor to be of more importance than the need for dusting, he was perplexed. How could he retain the one and accomplish the other? His ingenuity was being taxed to the utmost, and we find him sitting in his chair frowning with indecision, and measuring her wrath against his desire for tidiness.

Knowing her susceptibility to affection--every woman's weakness--his strained thinking turned to the possibility of fusing criticism with an expression of endearment; that is, coating a rebuke with honey.

Suddenly, a smile betokening the birth of an idea crossed his face. He rose from his chair, crossed the room to the piano--which item of furniture slumbered under the heaviest coating of dust--extended an index finger, and in a most legible fashion traced on its dusty surface this message: "I love you, dear!"

(Note: Also recommended as excellent procedure when mirrors and windows beg to be cleaned.)

7

Of a June evening, the very same evening, four girls in four different bedrooms in four different homes, looked at themselves in four lying mirrors with four pairs of approving eyes and were each charmed with the beauty they saw there. Each had dressed to attend the same party and dance that same evening.

At the party, each rendered disparaging appraisals of the other--in strictest confidence, mind you--and each reported to the maligned ones what was said of her and by whom. This done out of warm friendship, of course. Strangely then, why did it cause wounded feelings and tears? Why then did it result in confrontations? Each, taken to task, righteously denied having said any such thing, and heatedly accused the person who said they did of being a "dirty liar" in shrill tones and with unconvincing words.

On returning home, the four girls once more consulted four lying mirrors in four different bedrooms in four different homes and again saw there beauty and charm. Jealousy, they each decided had to be the motive for those nasty remarks. Far more accurate fair, and reasonable, each thought, were the opinions of four different romantically-intoxicated boy friends, spoken in passionate whispers in four different parked cars, in four secluded spots, after the party.

My, oh my! Are truth and beauty incompatible?

8

A Matter of Priorities: Rotary is a fine organization with worthy aspirations. Members of Rotary are expected to attend meetings regularly and contribute their time to projects sponsored by the club. I am a Rotarian. The Church is a divine institution which commands my time, and which reminds me weekly of my obligation to live my beliefs, and to support it with my gifts and my service. I am a Methodist. Marriage is an old and established relationship between man and woman. My marriage partner has the understandable and reasonable attitude that she is entitled to make demands upon my time. I am a docile husband. Earning a living is a necessity in our present society. In fact, it is a 40-hour-a-week imposition on my time, and I frequently give it more than this amount, shall I say, "out of zeal"? I am a teacher. Recreation and leisure are now recognized needs amid the tension and strain of today's hectic life. In fact, doctors frequently prescribe vacations in lieu of medicines, but for the same fees. I suffer from tension. To meet the demands of Rotary, the Church, work, marriage and relaxation forces me to establish priorities for my time. I am forced to travel a meandering line among them hoping to escape adverse notice in all quarters while continually feeling guilty because I cannot shine everywhere. I find myself stealing time from one to mend my situation in another, and I become more artful as I practice, collecting a bag full of justifications as a defense for the times when I am embarrassed, as I am sure to be. It is not a good thing for me to do, but occasionally I see myself engaged in this practice, feel ashamed, and double my efforts to meet all the obligations upon my time. But it is a losing cause; I cannot meet them all fully. Know me then for what I am...but don't tell me what I am, because I am sensitive.

9

I may not know my faults, but you do. If you are unaware of yours, I, or any number of others could oblige you. Dodging any attempt to explain just why we as individuals are stone-blind to our defects, I turn to pondering why it is that we derive such pleasure and comfort from identifying and discussing the faults of others. I wonder if it isn't because of our very real need to live contentedly with ourselves? Certainly, a battered ego is a pariah of a companion, and egos being so sensitively composed are bleeding targets, even for fair criticism. Building them back to pleasant companionship, once assaulted, is a necessity. The handiest of all self-serving means to that end is, we all know, the inking of the worth of those we live with and compete against. By use of this device we bolster our ego until, in our prejudice, we stand above them. Even when our egos are in good repair, this tactic is a reliable means of sustaining them.

Never doubt that I regard you with admiration: but, fortunately, enough short of perfection to serve my ego-restoring needs. And, I thank you for that, though I know that I am always available when you have such a need.

10 DEER HUNTER'S SPECIAL

Gun in hand, he moved stealthily to the perimeter of the forest, and peered hopefully into the opening that stretched some distance before him. With unbelieving eyes, he saw standing there the largest buck deer he had ever beheld. This giant, bearing a rack of antlers that would grace any trophy room, raised his head as if suddenly aware of danger. At this propitious moment he raised his rifle and fired. Down went the magnificent beast. His was the ultimate trophy.

Amazed at his success, he leaped forward to claim his prize, but entangled in the sheets fell headlong out of bed, and was rudely awakened from his dream.

11 SEQUEL TO THE DEER HUNTER

It had been a fruitless hunt. He was homeward bound, empty-handed. As the weary miles unfolded, that giant buck appeared and re-appeared in his thoughts. The incident was so clear in mind in every detail that it eventually became real to him, and by the time he reached home had become an actual occurrence, and was to serve as his escape from the humiliation of admitting failure in his quest.

"Did you have any luck?" was the question put to him next day.

"Sure did! Man, you shoulda seen the buck I downed. You wouldn't believe your eyes. His antlers were this wide (indicated by a spread of arms.) I musta only stunned him though. I stood there a'lookin' at him when he jumped to his feet, bowled me over, and took off like a rocket. I was so shook up I couldn't do nuthin'. Believe me, he was one for Ripley."

The question is: when the liar believes his own lie, is that lie a lie any longer? Is the truth ever woven from the threads of falsehood? Are you sure? You neither hunt nor fish, do you?

12 FAMILY LIFE

Try as a man will, there are always certain occasions in married life when even the most congenial of partners just do not see eye to eye. In my case it has to do with the weekly washing, which we still do the old-fashioned way by choice. Involved in our differences are such important decisions as what brand of detergent to use, how much of it, the height of the water level in the washer, how hot it should be, whether the clothes should be hung outdoors or inside, and how they should be folded.

Frankly, it is a sorry sight to behold that lovely, sweet-tempered light of my life become a tyrant over something so picayune, and all in the face of the best advice a man can offer. A woman bent on doing things the wrong way, come hell or high water, is a big stone to turn.

13 HAPPY NEW YEAR

Smokers are villains, liberated women are still women, kids have mastered parents, the police hadn't better shoot criminals, jerks have rights, criminals have more rights, morality is an unsnapped girdle, do your own thing, Congress harbors crooks, welfare cheaters do better than you do ----------

Can't you imagine some crab saying such preposterous things, intending to throw cold water on our high hopes for the New Year? How could he focus so intently on the bad while overlooking the good?

Ignore him, I say! Stress what is right about your world. Or better yet, tell me.

14 THE WINTER SCENE

The snowflakes, as they drift to earth in the frosty air, are large and lace-edged. They fall in the hovering stillness of a winter's night, upon a spacious clearing, upon the dense forest that encircles it, and upon the tiny settlement that nestles on its near edge. Smoke from a dozen chimneys rises there in long spiraling columns as fires within struggle to overcome the frigid draughts that filter intrusively through cracks and fissures, wickedly bent on overcoming human comfort. Dim light escapes here and there through grimy window panes, made attractive by frosty designs, wherein kerosene lamps appear to flicker off and on as the shadowy figures of children at play flash by.

It is cold, bitterly cold. Polar air hangs about the area in skulking fashion. Overhead, dark clouds scud swiftly across the sky in huge ragged patches, and when the pale moon shows its welcome face between them, the eye is deceived into believing that it is it, not the clouds, that is dashing across the heavens. During these brief intervals its illuminating beams transform this otherwise drab landscape into an awe-inspiring panorama of uncountable glints and sparkles, while simultaneously drawing long and eerie shadows behind each stump and boulder standing above snow level in the clearing. The trees themselves are upholstered with snow, and their limbs sag under its weight.

The silence too is oppressive. It sits upon the scene with a heaviness matching the icy grip of the cold, but seemingly poised to welcome a sound, any sound that will disturb its inactivity; and when, as if in response to that need, the sad howl of a wolf rolls out of the forest to resound against its black walls in what appears a vain attempt to prolong an existence foredoomed to brevity, anticipation is rewarded. Some moments later comes the sharp report of a falling limb, over weighted by snow, to ride the air waves and die in the distance. To the keen ear, all the while, faintly detectable, from the settlement's confines, like background music, can be heard the muffled laughter and gleeful shouts of rollicking children to wound the air superficially.

An hour passes, then comes an enchanted moment. The clouds sail away, a curtain lifted, and the glorious moon, riding free and commandingly, sheds its golden rays upon the spectacular beauty of this winter's night. Unveiled for admiration and awe is the diamond encrusted carpet of white draped wrinkle-free over all, and sparkling, scintillating in every direction in unspendable riches; and erecting turrets, dome-shaped, over each stump in the clearing giving it the appearance of a burial ground with hundreds of similar headstones, all monuments to the forest giants that had once towered above them in majestic sway.

Sadly, scenes of this extreme beauty, not uncommon in this north country's wintertime, are ephemeral creations. But nature stands undaunted by their transitory character, and can be relied upon to create others of equal or excelling character as early as the next night. She is indefatigable in plying her artistry, and without limit in ingenuity and variations of themes and designs.

When, in the early darkness of morning, brawny lumberjacks of the settlement pull on their heavy clothing in preparation for another day's toil, there is little doubt that the deeper snow and colder temperatures will induce them to grumbling at nature's indifference to their wishes, and her intransigence generally. In this mood, are they likely to notice the beauty that has so enthralled us? Being men, prosaic in disposition, intent upon grubbing out a living by hard work, the likelihood would seem to be minimal.

But wait! That man, with the axe on his shoulder who pauses at the edge of the clearing, he who is stroking his whiskered chin and casting his eyes around the semicircle within his vision. Can he be drinking in the beauty of the scene before adding his footprints to the desecration? Possible, wouldn't you admit?

As a matter of fact, there cannot be anyone posing under the guise of a human being who is entirely bereft of appreciation of beauty, wherever seen, or however appearing unless he be absolutely without heart and soul, which equates with being one of the living dead.

Ah, beauty! How you stir the human soul. How much you add to life. How you touch the tenderest chords in our being, and play upon them. What a civilizing influence you are upon us, and how would we die emotionally if denied your strong influence.

15 MAN VS. NATURE

When I came upon it, I thought: "Here is the very sapling I want, and I have the very spot for it. By making the transplant I can correct Nature's helter-skelter choice of location and beautify my landscape."

As I dug, I appraised with a disdainful eye the poor positioning of another of its kind nearby, giving it scant chance of survival.

Carefully I made the move, carefully I tended the transplanted sapling, happily I envisioned it grown to beautify the landscape, and in a vile temper watched it yellow and die as its counterpart, with all its disadvantages, flourished tauntingly only yards away. My failure and Nature's success were in such opposition that I found the situation unbearable. With a vengeance, I tore the dead transplant from its place, with an axe, cut the living tree, and burned both with an attitude hardly belonging to a rational person; but, in my weird reasoning, evening the score. If I can't, neither shall you.

16 MISCELLANY

While the FCC is berating television for its cigarette commercials, we wish it would look into another aspect of TV ads aimed not at corrupting the youth but at demoralizing the adult. In TV commercials, nothing good happens to anyone past the age of discretion. Watch the people in these ads for awhile. Teenagers invariably have great glistening teeth. Adults have dentures and denture breath. Boys switch hair grease and girls are glad. Men don't have hair. If they do, it is full of dandruff. Boys douse themselves with shaving lotion and wait to beat off the women. Older men are happy to find something that drains all eight sinuses. Young people have fun. Older people have nagging headaches. Young people spend all night wolfing hamburgers at amusement parks. Older people go to a nearby movie and have to leave because their stomach is killing them. Girls have blond hair full of body and boys nuzzle it. Wives have gray hair and their husbands won't take them dancing. Men work hard and get ahead, only to have some pimply assistant tell them they have bad breath. The teenage wife makes a cup of coffee and turns her husband into a sex maniac. The older wife washes, irons, mops floors and puts up with birds on the sink, and her husband comes home with a miserable headache and takes it out on her. Girls are always washing their hair. Wives are always washing dishes. Teenagers wear sneakers and sandals. Adults wear support hose. Teenagers rub each other with suntan oil. Adults rub each other with liniment.

17

Once upon a time there lived a man who grew up having six fingers on each hand without any idea of what to do with the extra members. He lived in a puzzled state, believing that his deformity could prove useful if only he could think of the right situation. But time passed, and he remained frustrated.

One day he attended a tent show and there saw a two-headed man on display. Feeling a comradeship with this person, he inquired of him what he did with the extra head, and was told that it was ideal for talking to oneself. He was impressed so he inquired further.

"What would you do if you had six fingers on each hand like me." The two heads conversed briefly, then one said:

"Get out of here, will ya. You freaks make us nervous!"

"Look who's calling who a freak," he said and left, and in a year's time moved to the Netherlands. It was here that he became a national asset around the dykes, preventing floods, six at a time.

18

Much confusion exists about the coming of fall. Some assume that it begins with the re-opening of schools; others, particularly those who "live life with gusto," will state positively that it begins with the start of the professional football season. Still others will equate it with the flocking of birds, the appearance of salmon in the rivers the color-change of leaves, the ripening of the corn crop, the first frost, pheasant season, or a hundred other such "signs".

Actually, the autumnal equinox is the determinant. This event occurs annually at that precise moment when the sun- which in reality stands still with reference to the earth - appears to move southward until it stands directly over the earth's equator; which movement is caused by the earth moving northward rather than the sun moving southward, even though to a person standing on the earth, it appears that the sun is moving southward as the earth moved northward, you see.

Now that you understand, go out and correct the many misimpressions that exist concerning the coming of fall within your circle of friends and acquaintances.

1978   19

Blackbirds--there must have been a million of them--were holding a convention in the trees near my home. Their raucous cawing attracted my attention. Observing, I realized that they were choosing the leader who would guide them south for the winter. The trouble was that each appeared to want that distinction, and I concluded that each was making more and more promises, and proclaiming its qualifications at the top of its voice. How the selection was made--and it was made, for they left in a body, confident that they were being well led, but actually heading north, and flying backwards -I can't imagine.

Their choice was stupid. The newly elected leader had fed them the most misrepresentations of fact and made the most promises it had no intention of keeping, and in doing so had swung the election in its favor.

Humans Notice: Election of leaders coming up soon.

20   1970

Say, friend, are you sure that you are worrying about all the things you should be worrying about? You are a concerned citizen, aren't you? I'm not referring to the usual worries, you understand. Things like car payments, church budgets, and cancer, but what about the critical things; pollution, the drug traffic, the right of dissent, abortion laws, the decline of morality, inflation, overpopulation, crime in the streets, the mistreatment of minorities, desegregation, the credibility gap, campus revolts, rubella, police brutality, hunger, poverty, the Vietnam war, civil rights, urban decay, juvenile delinquency, the ecological balance, the generation gap, traffic congestion, nudity and Tiny Tim's sex.

If this list has omissions or not, it should be apparent that you can't do them all justice even though all are legitimate reasons for worry. In the random way you are going about, it, you certainly are giving too much attention to some, and too little to others. What you need is someone to schedule your worries for you. For example, if you were on a schedule you could give five minutes to each of those I have listed, and it would only consume two hours of your day. This would enable you to sleep nights with the comfortable feeling that you were doing your part and showing proper concern.

Also, you are probably forgetting entirely some proper and fitting subjects for worry. This happens because the news media has a habit of concentrating on some and neglecting others. Have you, for example, worried recently about the Communist threat, the nuclear threat, is God dead, is California doomed, will the sun explode into a nova, or the Mafia? You see what I mean?

With fish smothering in sewage, the redwoods dying in foul air, birds drowning in oil, wild animals succumbing to D.D.T., top soil washing away, think of what I have said. Let me schedule your worries for you. My rates are as attractive as those of H & R Block and I supply you with the same security. If I am in error, I will do your worrying for you. Is it a deal?

21

We love them, we depend upon them; but we've never completely understood them. We consider them the weaker sex, but rely on their strength. Their companionship and affection support us through stress and strain. Unless it was our mothers, no one holds us in greater esteem, or sees us through less critical eyes. The longer we live with them, the more we rely upon them. Our male egos would suffer severely without the bolstering they provide. They are vital to us.

Now, I ask you, aren't you ashamed that all she had to wear was that "same old thing?"

1981   22 REFLECTIONS

The life of a man is but a thread that may be parted in innumerable ways from innumerable causes. We are not born into this world with any guarantee of longevity. How many times in the life of a man, who survives to old age, can a backward look revive memories of near fatal occurrences and events. Really, the mystery of it often resides in the unanswerable question: "Why have I been spared while others fell victim?" Some will give the credit to themselves; but others, like myself, will never have an answer, just appreciation of the fact.

23

You wouldn't abide it from your wife, your neighbor, your friend--or from the president for that matter. Then why is it that in a hospital you meekly and submissively yield to the outright tyranny that is practised there?

"Sign here-remove your clothing--remove all jewelry--roll up your sleeve--turn on your side--drink this-hold your breath-you may breathe now--drink no water--swallow this, etc,, etc."

Orders, orders, orders; all coming from hospital personnel, and all backed up by a prison warden's tone of authority commanding instant obedience. Tyrannical? You bet!

My recent experience is typical. First off, I was scared of what might be wrong with me, and equally fearful of what they intended doing to me. This gave them the edge immediately. Secondly, they ordered me to strip and gowned me in attire that only briefly covered my modesty, and leaked peeks at every angle and with every movement. This upped their advantage over me. Thirdly, they ordered me to drink a laxative that should have been bottled and sold to scour the scale from boiler pipes, and then predicted its results, and kept time by my reaction to it. They chuckled among themselves when I dragged my weakened frame back to bed, reduced to semi-invalidism from its potency, and nodded knowingly to one another as they checked the clock. Now I was a "thing", or felt like It.

Completely subdued, a piece of putty in their hands, I looked forward to the anesthetic as an escape from torture. Shaken back to awareness, I was eventually discharged after a lengthy procedure that I'd swear was adopted unaltered directly from a state prison manual.   On the trip home, I found myself unconsciously eyeing the rear-view mirror as if anticipating pursuit, recapture, and return to the tyranny I'd just escaped. It wasn't until I was safely inside the walls of my domicile that I relaxed and enjoyed the fact that they had failed to find a reason to keep me in their clutches. Blessed, I say, is he who pays his premiums and never needs to use his insurance.

                          24   1971

The growing of beards and moustaches is flourishing in the year of our Centennial, as it should be. The question that often arises in the minds of the wearers at this time is "should I keep this hirsute adornment after the Centennial is over?" Some, no doubt, are proud of what they have produced, and will consider this carefully. Others have raised a disappointment and will quickly decide. Still others will not make the decision alone--their amorous wives will force them to razor it off, or their teenagers will influence them to keep it. In my case, my wife has offered no protest, which might tell you something, nor do I have any teenagers in my household to threaten me if I cut it off, so the decision appears to be mine alone. I do not like wearing a beard; what I have grown does nothing for my ego, only reaffirming my advancing age, causes people to miss noticing me while fixing their eyes on my chin hairs, has caused me to be compared with every bearded person from Santa Claus to Ho Chi Minh, and brings me only "dutiful kisses from my loving wife of the briefest duration possible." As a concession to the youngsters I deal with in school and to my grandchildren, I have decided that I will shave off my whiskers, but let the hairs grow in my nose.

1983   25

He was a liar with a reputation. She was an advocate of truth and honesty. Of marriageable age, they met, and romance blossomed.

Nowhere in life are falsehood and exaggeration more productive than in romance. He was singularly prepared to be successful at it. She was a sponge for it. His hyperbole became truth, verifiable in her mirror.

Truth wedded falsehood. In due time the veil of romance was rent by the rudeness of daily living. She became disgusted by his lying ways. He became provoked and embarrassed by her demands for the truth. They considered divorce, but she now carried the fruit of their union in her womb, and in deference to the unborn, reconsidered.

She bore twins, a boy and a girl. The boy favored his mother and her attitudes. The girl was the apple of her father's eye, and became a worse liar than he. Thus the perpetuation of the species.

Where, oh, where is the ladder to the improvement of mankind?

1980   26 SCANDAL

It is reason enough for one to suspect a known fletcher, whispered to have poussetted clandestinely, to be guilty of flagitious behavior. It should then surprise no one to learn that she thereby acquired a bad case of ptyalism. If one is aware of her repeated attempts to obfuscate this evidence behind a smoke screen of sisyphean-like excuses, resulting in her exacerbating promiscuously and shamelessly, he should be further convinced.

Add to these revelations her wanton piscivorous appetite, that she has indulged in horoscopy at intervals, is said, on good authority, to perorate in the neuk, and in addition is rumored to keep a moquette in her bedroom; then he who still doubts that she is nothing other than a pixilated malapert, must be declared alert to flummery and impervious to charlatanism.

(Editor's Note: Confused? See p.227)

27   1961

The demands on a business or professional man's time are a significant factor in his ultimate accomplishment as an individual. All intelligent men have unfulfilled urges to explore the extent of their abilities in one or more avenues of human endeavor not related to their occupations, whether it be the trimming of hedges or writing symphonies. The rub is to find the time amid the hustle and bustle of making a living, rearing a family, serving one's fellowmen, performing one's civic duties and participating in the social affairs which encumber his days and nights.

It is a squeeze; take too much time from obligations to pursue personal aspirations, and you incur disapproval. On the other hand, take time from personal aspirations and attend to the aforementioned obligations and you lose as an individual.

A man is stymied by the order of living and his gravestone will bear down on his frustrations.

28   1961

I went to the switch box to turn off the light fuse, and found it possessed by hornets. The switch box belonged to me, and I was in no mood to honor squatter's rights; so I dispossessed the hornets of their comb and home right on the spot. Whereupon one of their number transformed himself into a jet-propelled missile and stung me by evading my windmill-like defense. This enraged me, and I took immediate revenge by throwing up a cloud of DDT, and stomping the fallen enemy to oblivion with my heel.

The slaughter continued until I had fulfilled my thirst for vengeance, and the ground lay covered with the dead bodies of all four of them, including the one who stung me--and his close relatives.

At this point I began to suffer from remorse, and I vowed that never again would I indulge in such an orgy of killing. After all, I thought, these were poor little creatures with no understanding of legal rights who were defending their home against the rightful owner by the only means at their disposal, and as I plucked the stinger from my arm and watched it swell and redden to a rich tomato color, I said to myself, "All stings are for the best."

Then I fell asleep and dreamed that Wyatt Earp called a meeting of all hornets, and made them leave their stingers at the door, and I awoke laughing, my arm sore from having broken all those stingers into bits.

1961   29

I was listening to the radio the other day when the announcer said, "Do you know the cancer signs?" He enumerated them one by one. Strangely enough I had them all so when he suggested "See your doctor right away," I headed for the office.

This time the doctor was in, so I began to tell him my symptoms, expecting the worst. The doctor shoved a thermometer in my mouth before I could list my troubles completely and said, "How many cigarettes do you smoke?" When I allowed as how I smoked a reasonable number he took the thermometer back and suggested I quit smoking. So far I'd gotten no advice more than my wife could supply free, and I observed mentally that doctors only read one side of a controversy. They obviously don't know that a cigarette company official offered convincing proof that cigarettes don't cause cancer, or that one guy I knew quit smoking to prolong his life, and was hit by a car.

Now there's a real menace to life and limb, the automobile. Yet I'm the only one I know who is advocating that we give them up. For some reason doctors are against smoking and socialized medicine, but not cars.

Certainly doctors are indispensable men. We realize this each time they go on vacation. We depend on them to see that we get full use of our Blue Cross and my respect for them is enormous. You heard me, enormous.

I just finished reading an article on heart disease and I'm sure that I've got it. I was going to be sensible and rush to the doctor as the article suggested, but darn it all, I enjoy smoking.

EPITAPH

He dodged the cars successfully
Was not by lightning hit
He's gone; the only reason
He smoked a little bit.

30   1961

The pile of shingles had lain on the ground for over a month when I pulled off the top few and uncovered a community of ants who immediately began carrying eggs to a lower level out of the sun's rays. Many were caught on the shingles I held in my hands and went up on the roof with me where they dropped off and scurried about in mad and futile effort to orient themselves. The chaos I had created in their otherwise peaceful community life had changed them in an instant from orderly business-like insects into confused and frantic individuals who dropped off the roof's edge, ran in circles, clambering over each other, or hurried about without purpose or regard to personal safety.

I watched their frenzy with disdain and condemned them for their stupidity, and then I thought of the atomic bomb. I wondered if radiation would be the only and greatest menace should one fall.

1961   31

The vastness of space is an exaggeration of reality. Where distances are measured in light years and dead stars shine on for centuries after they have ceased to emit light, the mind of man is quickly lost from understanding, and the mechanics of the entire system are too much for him to comprehend in their totality.

Men of centuries past stood on this terrestrial ball and falsely imagined themselves to be the center of the Universe. It was a flattering belief, and one that added to their own self-importance. When one man dared to state that this was an erroneous conclusion, he was subjected to the indignity of being forced to apologize and retract his statements. But as truth will, his beliefs triumphed, and man shrank from his imagined position as the center of the Universe, around whom everything revolved to the ignominious position of being an inhabitant on a speck of dust which moved around the sun, which in turn moved within a cloud of stars, which in turn moved in a cosmos of star clouds of which there seems to be no end or beginning and which stretch out to infinity.

Man has significance only in the eyes of his fellow men. From them he seeks friendship, companionship and association, and with them he has importance. "No man is an island unto himself."

1961   32

It is fall and the frost has been on the pumpkin. Nature is beginning to wield her paint brush upon the forests and hedges. The cornfields are turning brown and the pheasants are considering evasive tactics, because war for them is imminent. Many varieties of birds have disappeared from the area as if swept away by one swish of the broom.

In the world of men, heavier clothing is being hauled out of storage and donned against the chill wind that only recently was forgotten because of its long absence. Nature is de-coloring people of their summer bronze and the forests and hedges are beginning to beckon hunters. Pheasants are not scaring people, but people are scaring people and they are building bomb shelters at a rapid pace.

At this time of year--this particular year--men and pheasants have a common problem; decimation of their ranks is a looming possibility. Who knows who will get his first? The hail of shotgun pellets or the bomb blast, the lead poisoning or the radioactive fallout, the rent of flesh or disintegration.

Really, what's the choice? Is the hunter to be hunted?

Of men and pheasants. Poor pheasants! Men have so many advantages.

I am offering an attractive life insurance policy which will pay you one million dollars within five minutes after you are hit by an atomic bomb, and I ask you, can pheasants be so well protected?

33   1961

I would like to call your attention to the fact that few persons reach their graves today physically complete. Almost all have been surgically relieved of the traditional "pound of flesh" from assorted parts of their anatomy. Incisions are being made as rapidly as the knives can be honed to proper edge.

This makes me wonder how much a person could lose in the way of anatomy and still remain alive. Starting with tonsils and ending with vital organs quite a bit could go apparently. It makes one feel as if funeral directors should have a sliding scale for funerals depending on how much of the man they get, and the number of pall bearers should be in this relation also.

How sweet is life to the individual that he should care to preserve it at such costs to his physical being; or is this the wrong conclusion? Is it rather, how cussed the individual that he will suffer such physical torment and subtraction of anatomy for no other reason than to collect on his Blue Cross insurance?

How are you holding up friend?

1961   34

For all of memory the word "ain't" has been a grammatical nightmare which generations of teachers have fought with all the zeal of crusaders, and because of which, generations of errant students have paid endless numbers of penalties, all for the purpose of eventual eradication of this hated verb corruption. But in spite of all, "ain't" has persisted as if it were genetic in origin.

And now what happens? According to the newspaper, Webster's latest dictionary edition accepts the word and bestows respectability upon it. It appears to be complete capitulation in keeping with that popular philosophy: "if you can't lick 'em, join 'em."

As if the teacher's lot isn't hard enough already they must now about-face and condone the very thing that they have so long and so earnestly fought. Why, it's like embracing the enemy! It's heresy!

I care not what others may do, but as for me, "I ain't a gonna give in, no how."

1961   35

When you got down to it there really wasn't anything wrong with the boy. It was just that his tongue protruded from his mouth because it was too long and too large to be accommodated inside. It must be admitted that this made him look stupid, which drew many unkind, if honest comments, although at the same time it did evoke a kind of grudging admiration from other children his age who had to wipe their mouths with napkins after eating.

The boy progressed to young manhood normally in all other respects, at which time he suddenly attempted singing and became an immediate sensation. A new fad in vocalizing called the "slurp" was popular, and with the special asset which was his, our lad's rise to fame was meteoric. There were no slurpers to approach him. Teenagers adored him and hung weights on their tongues in an effort to emulate their idol. It soon happened that anyone in the teenage set seen about with tongue in mouth was branded a square, and no one was more normal than our abnormal lad.

All this made parents of teenagers choke with rage, and such comments as, "put your tongue in your mouth and get to bed," became commonly heard.

Soon enough tongues became stretched until there were slurp singers galore, and our lad became miserable, and complained that he was no longer called stupid, which proves that the greatest handicap of all is to be like everybody else-- just ordinary, and that it is much more satisfying to be abnormal than to have no identity at all.

36 1961

The highly contagious "deer hunting fever" has struck again. It is a strange malady that germinates in the belief of each hunter that he will look down the sights of his gun and see the mightiest buck that ever grew antlers. To realize this dream, extensive preparation must be made. Special clothing, license, gun, ammunition, food, shelter, gas, oil, map, compass, knife, binoculars, etc., etc., ad infinitum. All to be stowed in the car trunk or trailer and hauled to some remote section of the north land which the wily deer is known to haunt.

This will be done in the face of mathematical evidence that but one in four will meet with success and bring home the venison. A varying number will be shot, die of heart attacks, get lost, die in auto accidents, go broke playing poker, get plastered, die of asphyxiation, present the wife with grounds for divorce, suffer food poisoning, forget his gun, or be forced to take his wife along.

And when it is all over these peerless hunters will find it necessary to tell whoppers about their experiences ranging from the size of the buck they missed to the amount of money they spent in the vain quest of their prey, and when they return evil smelling and be-whiskered to bathe and shave, they will play once again the unhappy role of civilized men until next year's hunting season offers them release.

Yes, sir. What we need is a vaccine for "deer fever", a far more prevalent malady than polio.

The apple tree crouched like a wrestler, its massive arms straining to hold aloft the burden of fruit it bore. The summer sun, as days passed, dripped its brush across the scene; and when autumn came the glory of ripening was completed, and the luscious treasure seemed only to await the picking.

But no hand was turned to the harvesting, and the chill of the first frost loosed stems from their aching branches until the ground beneath became a crimson circle of Nature's richest bounty which the cattle grazing there found delectable.

If no concern was shown that such a profusion of beautiful fruit should sour the earth, or become fodder, it was because scarcely an apple from this tree, as perfect as it appeared, was perfect. Convening in infesting bliss, a myriad of munching worms were coursing where the pulp was sweetest, sickening human desire.

As apples continued to fall, one lone scabby orb clung tenaciously aloft, and slowly rotted to a reddish brown, becoming a wizened worm castle whose former tenants were long since embalmed in the fermenting juices. When at last the wintry blasts tore loose its firm grasp, and it dropped to earth with a mushy plop, this omega of the crop, this glob of refuse mothered the germ of life which, with the warmth and wetness of spring, sprouted to reproduce its kind. A reason for genuine thanksgiving.

It is a paradox that life renews itself in death; so commonplace as to escape attention. No minor miracle though, but a well laid plan in which mankind is but one fact amongst tomes of data. Thus it was in the uncontaminated pre-fission world we loved so well. And then, the bombs fell, and radioactive fallout settled over what remained, and in the post-bellum world we won by force of arms--I look now upon our pitiful, deformed progeny and rightly or wrongly find myself wishing, God forgive me, that life no longer renewed itself.

38   1961

Jason Jones was out of work--laid off. The pinch of adversity was upon him and his suffering was beyond comprehension. His Cadillac went first followed by his Hi-Fi set and when he had dispensed with all that he could let go he was unable to support himself in a manner to which he was accustomed; so he became bitter and his faith in democracy was shaken.

When his unemployment compensation ran out, and he had nothing left but his house and foreign car, his disgust with his unhappy circumstances reached a pinnacle, so he liquidated, sold everything, renounced his American citizenship, bought an island in the South Pacific and went there to live.

Once on his island he had the natives declare him king and applied for foreign aid from his native country, the U.S.A. Getting the cold shoulder to his first request he established diplomatic relations with the Russians, and was photographed embracing their envoy upon his arrival. When these pictures appeared in the American press he got his foreign aid in a hurry.

Now he basks in the warm sun no longer disillusioned, but firmly proclaiming his kingdom to be allied with the western world and violently opposed to communism. He is admired by his people, for whom he has done as much with his foreign aid as he has for himself. In appreciation, they keep his Cadillac well polished.

39   1961

It was one of those high-level conferences between East and West, not uncommon in recent years, but so unfruitful when measured in terms of progress toward solution of the cold war. Beginning with a politely cordial atmosphere and degenerating, as hours passed and charges and counter-charges flew, into something almost hostile, and until it was readily apparent that the oft arrived at stalemate was once more reached, and the pleas of the Ivan Petroviches and the John Joneses for peace would again be disregarded.

When both sides were smarting with the unfairness of the other, and tempers were short, and the arsenals of accusation and threat were momentarily exhausted an awkward silence ensued during which the antagonists eyed each other balefully, knowing without saying that they had come to a point in disagreement without escape.

It was here that the little child's sobbing broke the silence, and all attention was turned her way. Somehow she had wandered into the smoke-filled room unnoticed by the door guards, and afraid and lost, stood there with tear-stained face, crying loudly and uncontrollably.

Forgetting all, there was a rush to her side, handkerchiefs appeared to dry the tears and words of comfort flowed from East and West as if there were common understanding of what to do. Without a thought of argument or difference of opinion, the crisis was solved, and a smile appeared on the tot's tiny face which erased all the atmosphere of hostility so prevalent a few minutes earlier.

Almost as suddenly, when the child was comforted and its lost mother arrived, the conferees, realizing that they were compromising their positions as diplomats representing nations, almost sheepishly left the conference room to continue their negotiations another day under more favorable circumstances when the possibility of agreement was less likely to be a cause of embarrassment.

1961   40

The presents under the Christmas tree represented a sizeable sum of money, and when opened on Christmas morning would surely answer the desire for the good things of life. Multiplied many times, under many Christmas trees, they also represented a prosperous season for the world of business; but to Randy Smith, age 3, and his sister Mary, age 5, they were a test of endurance. Waiting for Christmas morning was almost more than either could endure. The anticipation, while delicious, was such a strain that excitement filled their pre-Christmas days and dreams troubled their usually unruffled sleep.

When fire engulfed the Smith home on Christmas Eve it was a miracle that the family escaped the holocaust with their lives. Rescued by the firefighters, Mrs. Smith stood weeping at the loss and Mr. Smith, while trying to comfort her, felt abject with despair. The children, carried to a neighboring house for safety, could be seen in the glow of the flames, peering out of the window, agonized with crying.

For some strange and inexplicable reason, although all of the rest of the house was destroyed and the living room partly gutted by the flames, the beautiful Christmas tree and all the presents beneath it escaped with but slight damage from the water sprayed on the building by the firemen and in the bleak morning light the tree and its presents appeared like a bright and shining oasis amidst a dark desert of charred remains.

The Smiths retrieved their presents, and the children enjoyed them. All enjoyed the most meaningful Christmas they would ever enjoy, because the gifts of life and health, the most valuable of all, had been preserved to them.

41   1962

Nostalgia must cause you to think occasionally of that pale orb, the moon, which in our day "Came Over The Mountain" to shine on "Pretty Red Wing" in the vicinity of "Moonlight Bay". But it's no longer the same old moon that shone through our Model-T windshield as we promoted our teenage romances with fumbling success; and whose candlepower bathed us in light just bright enough to hide our embarrassment. Nor is it the same old moon by which the farmer gauged his planting, the robber his second-story depredations, or the lunatic his mad dances. The new generation seldom heed the moon, and certainly seldom consider it an adjunct to romance of the same caliber as a drive-in movie.

Today the moon is a celestial body of minor significance off which we bounce radio signals, at which we aim rockets, and concerning which we envision a way station for interplanetary travel.

It is already scarred by a Russian rocket and ignored by sky watchers in favor of the Echo satellite, and it has become a factor in the mad race for space real estate.

There is no loss without some gain, 'tis said. In this case I am sure that the loss is great and the gain dubious. It was a fine old moon, and so functional in the old days. The only regret we ever had at that time was that one moon had to suffice for us while the favored planet Jupiter had a luxurious twelve, and no model T's to shine upon. A really very unproductive circumstance.

1962   42

The wind blew and the trees bent, the water roared down the rivers and boulders creaked and stirred, the lightning flashed and rent the air, while cascades of water descended in a torrent. It was a miserable night for man and beast.

The fact that Andrew was out in all this foul weather was the result of a choice he had exercised. If his election seemed unwise and ill-considered you must weigh the alternative. You see, he had a warm comfortable home which shed water and turned back the wind, and was protected against lightning. But in this warm, dry and comfortable home was his wife of many years, Bella, whose momentary attitude toward the aforementioned Andrew, her husband, was more fierce in his estimation than the storm outside. Thus the choice or lack of it, depending on your marital experience.

The lightning that darted from her angry eyes, the words that poured in a torrent from her snarling lips, and the niagara of tears that were poised to flow at the instant of desire, were simply more fearsome to Andrew than the blasts of nature outside, so he sloshed along dripping water and crouched against the wind hoping to be struck dead by the next lightning bolt.

The incident which touched off this crisis was commonplace. At supper the fried potatoes were burned, they lacked salt and they tasted of the fish fried in the grease. The mistake which Andrew had made was merely that of saying what was obvious - the fried potatoes were burned, they lacked salt and they tasted of fish. What reckless disregard for his personal welfare had led him to utter these fatal words is hard to understand. Andrew was not a newlywed and should have known better.

Nature's fury will end - this can be predicted, but Andrew must face the storm at home, sooner or later. Let the poor fool drown, I say, it serves him right!

43   1962

All his life he had been a collector, probing for new items which intrigued his fancy, and which could be carried home and placed among his growing museum of trivia. No item was too insignificant to merit his inspection, or rate consideration for a place amid the jumble of litter which was his treasure.

As this treasure grew his concern for its safety against incursions by neighbors became greater and greater, and occupied more and more of his time. Like any miser he hovered over his booty to protect it from the greed and envy of others, and thus was prevented from the continued pursuit of his love of collecting.

In his effort to protect what he had, he gradually became more and more fierce, snapping at all who dared to approach his abode to cast a covetous eye. The more time he gave to protecting his treasures, the more he attracted the attention of others to its desirability, and as greed grew in his neighbors, fear of pirating grew in him.

Soon enough every minute of his time was taken up with vigilant and militant guard duty, and even the necessities of life had to be ignored. He became gaunt from hunger and red-eyed from lack of sleep, and ready to jump at the rustling of a leaf. He no longer had friends, only enemies.

Finally, exhausted from inattention to his personal needs, he could no longer continue his vigil. It was then that he dragged his wasted body from his home in search of life-giving food. But, alas, it was too late, and while attempting to cross a rubbish pile he expired, never to know how quickly his relatives and neighbors plundered his cache, nor ever to be subjected to the unfeeling comment of a passerby who, viewing his wasted remains, was heard to remark, with merciless lack of regard for the dead: "One less pack rat."

The rocket took off with a swoosh, and began its pioneering voyage into the far reaches of outer space. The astronaut inside was rapt in awe at the view of the universe unfolding before him, and how he happened to notice the frog hopping around his cubicle is a question worth asking.

"How in the world did a frog get into my spaceship?" thought the astronaut as his ship passed into the ionosphere where, strangely enough, men and frogs are able to communicate by thought wave. Startled when the frog began to answer him the spaceman nevertheless listened intently.

"Why am I here?" said the frog. "It's this way. I lived in a quiet pond as did my ancestors before me, and one day as I dozed in the sun on a lily pad several distraught relatives of mine rushed up to inform me that one of our more promising tadpoles had been devoured by a snake. Now we could spare one tadpole, but all this croaking drove me to the thought, 'why not do something about the snake menace?' So I organized a vigilance committee on the spot, and set up an alarm system to warn all frogs in the pond of the snake's movements."

"Are you with me?" asked the frog, "Yes, indeed," said the spaceman, "go on!"

"Well," said the frog, "the success of my plan was simply amazing. Our mortality rate fell to a point where I would have suggested birth control had I understood it, and amid the new security my relatives did some thinking of their own, and plead with me to extend the system to other ponds in the area. So I sent missionaries to all points with an ample supply of pamphlets on 'Successful Tactics for Evading Snakes'. After this I can't imagine what snakes did for food, but frogs went off their diet."

"Then the trouble began."

"Trouble?" said the spaceman, "tell me about it."

"It was a case of upsetting the balance of nature," said the frog, "idleness begot the begats, if you know what I mean, and frogs were everywhere and everyone of them croaking curses for me and my plan. I had to take it on the lam to save my life and retain my sanity."

At this point the frog did a few back flips and spun around like a top, laughing uproariously all the while, and then said: "That's why I'm here! I'm crazy! And now, Mr. Spaceman, tell me, if you're not crazy, what in hell are you doing here?"

45   1962

I just can't understand all the to-do about John Glenn spending 5 hours in space. It's an affront to our family that Uncle Oscar, who as you know, spent several months in space a year or so ago, received no such acclaim. Why people are so partial and unfair in this matter puzzles me. Just compare statistics, if you will. What are three revolutions around the earth compared to months of touring the far reaches of the Universe? And this exorbitant expenditure of 300 million dollars by the government to accomplish so little when for $595.98, on the Sears, Roebuck discount plan, Uncle Oscar performed a miracle. If this doesn't represent a rank injustice I never heard of one.

Of all of Uncle Oscar's outstanding feats, his tour of space stands as the only one the family can look upon with pride. Nor was it any less of a miracle because Uncle Oscar wouldn't divulge his findings to the government. In fact, I came to support him in his obstinate refusal. Why should he tell what he discovered when the agencies who requested to know were the very same who denied him assistance in his project, forbade him to take the trip, declared his homemade rocket ship a death trap, and took him into custody on his return.

There is no place any longer for the tinkerers like Uncle Oscar who got the Machine Age underway, I swear if Henry Ford had been born fifty years later he would have lived in obscurity. I'd write my congressman only I doubt the worth of it.

Humph! Big deal! Excuse me while I put some flowers on Uncle Oscar's grave.

Imagine if you will a vast reservoir, capable of holding all of a valuable commodity that the people of the world could generate, the capacity of which has never been taxed in the least. The outlet of this huge reservoir is constantly busy from withdrawals by individuals, but the inlet is only intermittently visited for replenishing. Behold that the level of the contents varies little, and surmise correctly that the few replenishers return large amounts sufficient to cover the many withdrawals. Be informed that the contents have the rare property of increase by use, and deduce properly that those who withdraw a portion of the valuable contents and put it to use by sharing it, multiply the amount many times over, while those who withdraw, but fail to put it to use, lose what they took, and have nothing to return. Conclude wisely, that since the contents are of great value to men, it is highly desirable to increase the total, which can only be accomplished by more withdrawals, not less; more use of the contents, not less, and more returns, not fewer. Ask me why mankind is not busy taking, sharing and returning, and I can't answer the question other than to state that, like money, this commodity is easily squandered by hoarding, and has a short life if not soon shared or put to use in one way or another; and so many men accept it without thought of sharing it or passing it on that much of it evaporates, or disappears. Somehow the substance is so easy and enjoyable to receive and so difficult to part with that few find its secret of "increase by use", or ever learn that use of it multiplies satisfaction and pleasure.

And what does this vast reservoir contain, you ask. Well, Shakespeare lamented its loss when he said of men, it is "oft interred with their bones." It is, of course, G-O-O-D-W-I-L-L.

When at birth the doctor slapped me and I gave voice to a lusty yowl, I became a critic of the world into which I was born. It was that easy. My special talent was destructive criticism, and never in all my years has my ability to produce it forsaken me. Yet, as I grew and criticized, I hated to have the same withering breath blown on me that I was ever so ready to breathe on others. Why it was like this I have never really understood excepting to decide that it ran deep into human nature which psychologists say has not changed noticeably in the last 30,000 years.

Though I knew this, as a young man I set out to prove an old adage wrong. When I heard it said that "you can't please everybody" I was too idealistic not to challenge it, but after I suffered numerous bitter experiences, and my best intentions had been dashed to pieces by my critics, I regretfully yielded to this cliche and acknowledged to myself the perverseness of human nature.

I notice that other persons take this lesson in different ways, Some defiant of it continue to fight a losing battle; some compromise with it and are satisfied with majority approval; others are beaten by it and declare that they have no concern with approval or disapproval.

But I wonder if the old Quaker didn't have the best solution when he said to his wife, "Mary, everybody is queer but me and thee, and sometimes I think that thou art queer also." Such sublime conceit is impervious to the sharpest criticism, and the perfect insulation against all criticism.

48   1962

The youngster was bored with inactivity. He was tired of his bicycle, the TV set, his parents and their rules. He'd seen the movie, games were too childish for him. He wanted a car, complete freedom of action, spending money, and no advice or restriction.

While I was feeling sorry for him I got to thinking of my youth, how much I enjoyed it, and wondered that I couldn't recall being bored at all.

I wouldn't dare suggest to a youth with today's advantages that he try the things I did for fun and adventure. I know he wouldn't care for hikes in the woods looking for slippery elm bark, or spruce gum to chew; walking miles down the railroad tracks after wild flowers or interesting stones; going to the mill to sack corncobs to peddle at 5¢ a bag for spending money; visiting the depot, putting a penny on the railroad track and hunting for it after the train passed by; riding on the dray or with the groceryman on the delivery wagon; fishing with a bent pin for a hook; catching butterflies with a mosquito netting device of my own invention; making and flying kites; rolling a hoop; skating on the sidewalk; playing marbles; damming up the creek with rocks and mud to make a swimming hole; trapping muskrats; hunting the countryside for hickory nuts, beechnuts, walnuts or butternuts; putting hairs from a horse's tail in the rainbarrel to make "snakes"; taking the BB gun to the dump to shoot rats; visiting the slaughter house; working the bellows for the blacksmith's forge, or digging caves in the sand bank.

What delicious pleasures these things were, and none of them requiring money.

Do you think kids have lost the secret of fun?

1962   49

I have eight acres of hilly land which grows only undesirable trees that proliferate at a pace difficult to restrain. As a matter of fact, it was while cutting away at this undesirable growth that the idea first occurred to me. It was an obvious moneymaker, and the terrain lent itself well to the need; but I couldn't get any information on how to go about giving the idea reality.

What I am looking for was a "do it yourself" plan for starting a cemetery. I could envision my acres flourishing with graves and headstones, and sprouting flowers and shrubs while my bank account climbed.

But, how does one start a cemetery? Would it do to advertise "Beautiful location for your last resting place?" How does one get the hearses headed in the direction of his new cemetery? Can he properly offer a special inducement like "two for the price of one"? This is a delicate area, and one that can only be handled with tact and good taste.

I'm stymied! I fancy that the bereaved have some aversion to planting their "dear departed ones" in an "uninhabited" surrounding, and if this be true I repeat my question: "how does one start a cemetery?"

Really, the only way I can see open for starting a cemetery is to die myself and become the first occupant, and this way, gentlemen, eliminates all the inducement.

Oh, well! Back to cutting trees!

50   1962

Let me say immediately that I am not morbid, and the thought of dying has never seemed the least inviting to me. Considering myself a condemned man awaiting execution, as I have done so many times, is merely an exercise in imagination, not a hoped for reality. Of course, to induct myself into the proper mood I must, and do, follow through all the aspects of the predicament as they have been so often and so vividly displayed in movies and on television.

I have never really considered it important why I was condemned to die, excepting to feel, vaguely, that it was a frameup, or I had been falsely accused, or at the very least that I was an object of extreme pity.

Each time I have walked the "last mile" it has been with dignity and courage, such that many an executioner has quailed at pulling the trap door on me, or turning on the "juice" to do me in. My utterances on these occasions have been terse, but classical in worth, and my proud bearing, and the enigmatic smile on my lips at the fatal moment have both failed the attempts of the best artists to recapture on canvas.

I have died a thousand deaths, and for what purpose? Well, honestly, that's the intriguing element of a bizarre circumstance surrounding an execution which lures me through this sequence of events again and again. In no other way can I place myself in an ultimate position where I have this one choice to make, and only this one, and wherein the failure to make it satisfactorily will not allow for correction.

I, of course, repeat the experience again and again in my imagination so that I may repeat the opportunity of trying for complete satisfaction which, so far, I have never attained. Truthfully, I just cannot decide, for all the attempts I have made at it. I am becoming frustrated!

If you were a condemned man what would you order for your last meal?

1962   51

We should be awed by the wonders of modern living. Here I sit, cozy in my warm living room, watching television. The movie I am watching is about the vanished American Indian, the Redskin. It comes to my living room through the ether with the speed of light (for the second time). What a contrast in eras; modern television, and the crudity of Indian life.

The story depicts an Indian scout cautiously observing a wagon train of hated palefaces moving into a canyon. As the scout scurries about in search of wood to light a signal fire so that he may communicate with the band of braves beyond the hill, who are painted and ready to attack, I step to my telephone, another of those marvelous modern inventions, and lift the receiver preparatory to calling a friend a few blocks away.

Whoops! The line is busy. Those palefaces across the street no doubt.

Back in the living room I observe the Indian scout kneel and strike flint against steel over his fagots. What a laborious process this is for making communication over a distance just a whoop and a holler away, I think to myself. Again and again he brings forth sparks until, after what seems an eternity, the fire is ignited.

Five minutes later his signal fire has only begun to burn as I again lift the receiver of my lightning-like means of modern communication to call my friend.

Oh, oh! Still busy! Well, back again in my living room I observe the Indian scout who finally has his fire blazing, piling green leaves upon it to create a cloud of smoke which he begins to manipulate with his blanket into a series of decipherable puffs and wisps. The warriors charge, and scalps are dangling from their belts as the toothpaste ad comes on the screen. Well, I'll be darned! Someone else has the line! Yes, sir.

Today's rapid communication is a marvel of technology. The telephone is an indispensable part of modern living and a great boon to the paleface. It is a supreme triumph for civilized man over the barbaric ways of the Indian. Darn it all! The line is still busy. Oh, well! I'll try again at dinner time when there's a chance that the phone won't be in use.

52   1962

Not more than a yard away lay a piece of binder twine which was just the ticket for repairing the damage done when, with one Herculean effort, he had dislodged the stone from its resting place and simultaneously, by this prodigious effort, broken the belt on his trousers. He could see the piece of twine clearly enough, and certainly knew how to use it to keep his trousers up, but with one hand holding them from dropping to his heels, and the other balancing the boulder which teetered precariously on the ledge of earth at head level, the problem he faced was complicated. He could, of course, let his trousers fall, free one hand, and by an acrobatic maneuver, just grasp the sorely needed piece of twine; or he could put both hands to the boulder and move it to a stable position on the ledge where the danger that it would topple on him would be removed.

Unfortunately his dilemma was greater than it appeared. Not a hundred yards away at the clothes line stood the neighbor lady, whose hearing was seriously impaired at middle age, but whose eyesight had suffered no degeneration.

It was a difficult choice he had--lose his modesty or impair his well-being. Actually, the time he had for making the decision was not as long as it seemed, for the arm supporting the wobbling boulder was rapidly tiring from the strain, and he dared not change hands. You wouldn't believe it, but things turned out all right and he gets around quite well now with the use of a cane.

For decades they have stood against the horizon, seemingly as permanent as the sky itself, their long arching limbs sweeping out symmetrically and gracefully from sturdy trunks. They have lined the roadways and fence lines of the countryside and have stood high in majestic sway over the roof tops of village homes like giant umbrellas providing shade against the hot summer sun, and they have stood outlined in gold as the sun dropped behind them to end a day. Birds have found their branches welcome resting places from flight and have gossiped in their leafy crowns or held sessions on territorial rights high up in their stretching arms. Squirrels used their limbs as pathways for travel and many a farmer has sought the shade of their branches as respite against the heat of the day.

The once mighty elms are succumbing to disease first and the biting teeth of the chain saw next, and are thudding to earth, already dead or dying, leaving only a broad stump to mark their place, and a few to sing their elegy in a day when the destruction of Nature's treasures is almost a national practice.

The loss of these patriarchs is leaving great gaps in the familiar scenery. There is no question that it would take a lifetime to replace their loss and probably they will never be replaced. The woodsman's saw earlier felled the virgin forests and created a permanent change as farm fields took their place. Perhaps today's loss of the elms will mean a permanent lowering of the skyline which has for so long stretched to the topmost branch ends of the passing elms.

"Sic transit gloria mundi"

1962 54

I have recently returned from a foreign country so thinly populated that an hour's drive took me into a complete wilderness where crude dwellings made of logs were found along the shores of lakes, and wherein the inhabitants were forced to walk or paddle a canoe go get about.

Other unspeakable privations had to be endured along with the lack of roads. The absence of electricity, running water, proper sewage facilities, stores, doctors, schools, banks and similar essentials added to the inconvenience of life here in this wilderness which, although it abounded in game and fish, required men to engage in the exhausting processes of hunting and fishing to get it.

Fuel was plentiful, but lay strewn about the landscape with no regard for ease of collection, and once collected had to be reduced to size with an axe or saw to be usable. Even then it required slow ignition before yielding its heat energy in quantities and at a rate hard to control.

The scenery was monotonous, consisting mostly of an unending forest of towering trees with intervening lakes of crystal clear water, and noisy streams which coursed among rocks creating at places a din of gurgling, bubbling and roaring which took the place of the familiar music of automobile traffic. Also to be endured were the trilling, whistling, chirruping and singing of numerous colorful birds who constantly flitted amongst the foliage, and most particularly, the loons complaining wail which often continued after darkness and was a distinct deterrent to restful sleep.

Animals roamed about this wilderness unrestricted and with an offensive air of ownership, emphasized by their huge size in some cases, and their sharp teeth and claws in others. Some times they completely ignored my presence, and at other times displayed an equally irritating tendency to drive me away.

The air was mostly odorless, and its harmful effect on the lungs was negligible. Flowers which grew indiscriminately across the landscape as if a careless gardener had sown them, added a fragrance to the air. The water in the lakes and rivers was almost transparent and men were forced to drink it because of the total lack of a treated supply.

Such a mess! Pure air, pure water, unadulterated landscape, roaming wild life, scenic lakes, coursing streams. Something should be done for the poor souls who must live their lives and rear their families in such a forsaken place. Thank heaven for civilization!

POEMS

PEACE (1969)

Peace is an interlude 'twixt wars,
When wounds heal,
And young lads come to might
In whom the will to fight
Knows no repeal.

Young lads whose fathers went to war
Across the sea,
And spent their blood in vain beau geste,
Engaged upon the noble quest
That peace might be.

Peace is the dream that stirs the brave
To carry arms,
Whose passions flame at every call
Who dash to battlefields and fall--
The gallant ones.

Peace is the balm that cannot soothe
The brutal man,
Whose ugly appetite for hate
Demands he kill or devastate
With sword or pen.

Peace is a plot in foreign soil,
Our hero's bed,
Who in his slumber cannot know
What causes of a new war grow
Above his head.

Peace is every mother's prayer,
Who's borne a son
To face the tocsin's beck'ning call,
Or sobbed before the coffin's pall:
"Thy will be done."

Peace is He who calmly turned
The other cheek;

Forgave his enemies; was slain
Upon a cross, that we might gain
The peace we seek.

To Sally (1969)

If I admire someone,
And friendship blooms,
There is no doubt
I lay upon myself a future sadness
When that tie runs out.

For friendship starves from separation,
And becomes a gaunt recollection
Of a former time and place,
With dissipated warmth,
And acquires a musty odor
From being relegated
To the attic of the mind.

Store me gently among your recollections
I've admired you.

Modern Problems

Hang up your stocking
It's that time of year
Santa is coming
To fill them, my dear,

Now, Jennie, you know
You're not being fair.
Why are you hanging
Those leotards there?

Chance

Chance, the gambler's flirtation with the odds;
The foolhardy lad's impulse to derring-do;
The adventurer's thrust to great discovery;
The maiden's trust her lover will be true.
Chance, the hero's doorway to beau geste;
The prisoner's happenstance to safely flee;
The soldier's prayer amid the hail of fire;
The sailor's hope to sail a favoring sea.
Chance, a circumstance beyond foretelling;
Inherent in the Creator's master plan;
A lottery begun with life's inception;
Nor Adam knew what was in store for Man.

Florida

Florida, Florida
Look who's gone to Florida,
The feeble, whom the wind blows through
The idle-rich, with naught to do,
The devotees of shuffleboard,
Those who can't the trip afford,
Others who have boats to sail
Some for tans, whose skin is pale,

Divorcees, who are on the prowl,
Retirees with a sagging jowl,
Through the traffic jams they go
To escape our winter's snow,
But we'll stay come hail or blow
Standing to our knees in snow,
Believing that our ordeal should
Clearly prove our hardihood.

THE MEDICINE SHOW

(circa - 1920)

The Medicine Show has come to town,
Handbills on every post,
It's an annual occurrence,
To which our town plays host.
They draw a fair-sized audience,
And of a cureall boast,
But the want of some diversion,
Attracts its patrons most.
Some will brand them swindlers,
The gullible to bilk,
Others are equally confident,
They are not of that ilk.
Those who cast suspicion about,
Before these shows commence,
Could be convicting without proof,
And shy of evidence.
I am, by nature, a trusting soul,
My friend is otherwise,
He brands them shysters, and asserts,
"Fleeced is the one who buys."
I say, "attend before you judge,
Prejudgment is a bad idea."
Myself, I'm certain what they sell
Is a genuine panacea.
Still, I am very much bothered by
The attitude of my friend,
To vindicate my own beliefs,
I've decided to attend.
The hour comes for the show to start,
Music issues its call,
A banjo is playing a lively tune,
As I enter its canvas walls.
The music ends, a salesman comes,
He stands on a stage of planks,
The audience is taking seats,
In chairs set up in ranks.

A hush falls over the audience,
As the salesman begins to speak,
The words come out of the side of his mouth,
Which I think is rather unique.

——— o ———

"Welcome," he says, "good ladies and gents,
Enter, come one, come all,
Don't hesitate, come right on in,
Should you walk, or run, or crawl.
Seat yourselves as suits you best,
Up front if you're hard of hearing,
All should hear of our miracle cure,
The end of pain is nearing.
Make Way! Here comes a gentleman,
Obviously wheelchair bound.
Provide him with a front row seat
On firm and solid ground.
Pull out a chair, and wheel him there.
Sympathize with his plight,
Show him every courtesy,
It's nothing more than right.
Now, give me your attention please,
Lend me all your ears,
I've got a story to relate,
Untold for a thousand years.
Driving one day in the desert's heat,
My car gave out on me.
I could only walk and hope that I
Would survive this calamity.
I lost my way, and wandered far,
Doomed to a horrible fate,
When amazingly I blundered upon
A ruin of ancient date,
Just as I thought each step my last,
That death was near at hand,
Expecting to find my lonely grave,
There in the blistering sand.
An indian ruin apparently,
Hidden by canyon walls,

Where life had flourished abundantly
In ages beyond recall.
What had become of its residents,
Had they died or fled,
Little was left to indicate,
Just eerie silence instead.
I thought at first it was a mirage,
Renewing all my fears,
But water in plenty was bubbling up
As pure as your lady's tears.
Refreshed, my curiosity grew,
I took a look around.
That's when I spotted a mysterious stone,
A sticking out of the ground.
I wrested it from the sandy soil,
And painted on its face,
Were symbols whose meanings perished, I thought,
With men of that ancient race.
How I got home is foggy detail,
My wife has since told me,
I was clutching that stone within my arms,
Babbling incoherently.
Later I found an interpreter
Who could read what the symbols said,
Once himself a proud young Chief,
But now of shuffling tread.
Through rheumy eyes he strained to read
What amounted to a cure,
For all those annoying miseries,
That humans must endure.
I made the concoction as prescribed,
And tried it on myself,
It was so effective I came to keep
A bottle on my shelf.
I winced when a friend accusingly said,
'You're selfishly inclined,
Why don't you bottle and sell this stuff,
For the benefit of mankind?'
Now, that's my reason for being here,
With my blend of herbs most rare,

The demand is great, as you can guess,
It's wanted everywhere.

————— o —————

I heard this tale somewhat in awe,
Sharing his misery,
As if I'd traveled with him to make,
His great discovery.
I found no element of deceit,
In what he had to say.
I thought it entirely plausible
To have happened in this way.
But the salesman in continuing on,
And deserving of our attention,
If I've diverted you, momentarily,
Excuse the interruption.

————— o —————

"Our supply is very limited,
As luck would have it be,
But we have enough to satisfy
This small community.
But, more important is what it does,
And that you're entitled to know,
So you can decide independently,
If you choose to buy, or no.
One bottle of this miracle cure,
Can stop your aches and pains,
It's useful for removal of
Ink and gravy stains.
It's earned a reputation for
Preventing falling hair.
It can't be beat for cuts and sores,
Apply it anywhere.
A single bottle of our cure,
Provides 'get up and go'
If that were less than proven fact,
I'd certainly tell you so.
I lay the truth before you all
Against opposing claims.

For testimony of this fact
I'll produce a hundred names."

———— o ————

Suddenly he interrupts his spiel,
Unnerved by a noisy crank,
He's trying to hold his temper in check,
As he paces on the planks.
Finally, somewhat calmed he gives
His taunter an ugly glare,
Who happens to be, surprisingly,
That cripple in his wheelchair.
The salesman's ready to respond, I see,
That we won't want to miss,
All are straining their ears to hear,
So let's tune in on this.

———— o ————

"Now, Sir. You in the wheelchair there,
You've constantly heckled me,
I'll ask you very civilly,
Desist out of courtesy.
You say I do not speak the truth,
You mimic me and jeer,
It's your prerogative, I suppose,
But, please don't interfere."

———— o ————

I thought the salesman had handled
That situation well,
In gentlemanly fashion, I would say,
Which should help his product sell.
He goes back to selling right away,
His heckler well chastised,
If he doesn't keep his big mouth shut
I'll really be surprised.

———— o ————

"Now folks, back to our miracle cure,

One dollar price is cheap,
Step up and get your bottle now,
It's benefits to reap.
A tablespoon at bedtime will
Insure a night of rest,
There's nothing better to be had,
When tired and depressed.
I'll list some actual instances,
Documented in our files,
As proof our miracle elixir
Changed suffering to smiles.
When Sam Hill was bedridden,
He drank a bottle down,
Now he's up cavorting with
Pretty Nellie Brown.
Take the case of Widow Crumley,
When the doctor shook his head,
Implying her chances were hopeless,
And she as good as dead.
One glass of our elixir put
Her back upon her feet,
Last week she was remarried to
A gent from down her street."

——— o ———

The salesman is annoyed again,
Wrongly I'd supposed,
That wheelchair gent was squelched enough
To keep his big mouth closed.
But no, his big mouth was busy again,
Tossing insults anew,
The audience was irritated,
With boos from one or two.
How will the salesman handle this?
Words won't clear the air,
To muzzle this tormenting jerk
He'll need a club, I swear.
He's looking rather confident,
Got something up his sleeve,
If he gets blunt and downright mean,

Maybe the guy will leave.

———— o ————

"You're more and more obnoxious, Sir,
You're getting in my hair,
Must you question all I say?
You're being most unfair.
I'll tell you what I'm goin' to do,
I'll give you a bottle free,
If you'll promise to drink it all,
And report the result to me.
You say our cure is worthless,
You say I'm telling lies.
Try it, I say, and you may be
In for a big surprise.
Return again tomorrow night,
Then let us hear your story,
If I'm the liar you say I am,
You be my judge and jury.
Take this bottle without a charge,
No longer be in doubt,
Know for yourself what it can do,
And cast uncertainty out."

———— o ————

The wheelchair gent is trundled out,
Grumbling as he goes,
The bottle of elixir in his hand,
But where to, no one knows.
The salesman's clever maneuver,
Earned him my respect,
I now was sure his honesty
No longer was suspect.
This incident had ill effect,
Sales were in decline,
So the salesman faced his audience,
Having made up his mind.

———— o ————

"That ends our show for tonight, good friends,

Come early tomorrow to see,
Our little dancing dog do tricks,
To the tune of Rosalee.
Our wheelchair critic should return,
His verdict you will hear,
Then you will know as well as he,
The worth of our elixir."

——— o ———

Decision time comes rolling 'round,
The crowd o'erflows the tent,
The little dog performs his act,
To the general merriment.
But, where, oh where, is the wheelchair gent?
Expectation is running high,
Has he chosen to not appear?
All are wondering why.
The show is quickly underway,
Two bottles for a buck,
But sales are lagging noticeably,
For all that bargain struck.

——— o ———

"Step right up. Get your supply."
The salesman pleads in vain,
"Here's a bargain you can't turn down
Unless you covet pain.
What's that ruckus in the rear?
Who's making all that din?
Can it be! Would you believe!
It's that wheelchair gent again.
But look! He's walking down the aisle,
What a wonderful surprise,
A miracle is happening,
Before our very eyes."
The audience is mesmerized,
They stand in awe to look,
Then cheers ring out so lustily
The very tentstakes shook.
Down the aisle at a halting pace,

The former cripple walks,
Shouting praises of the cure,
Last night he had downtalked.
"Come to the fore," the salesman said,
"What has taken place?
Explain this transformation, please,
Tell us face to face."

——— o ———

Help he got to mount the stage,
Beside the salesman stood,
Extolled the virtues of the cure,
As very well he should.
This rejuvenated crippled man,
This noisy carping critic,
Stood before this audience,
Would he dare admit it?
That he was out of line to say,
The harmful things he'd said?
Has he the guts to apologize,
And hang his shameful head?

——— o ———

"Look at me! A new man now,
I stand upon my feet,
Would you believe that just last night
I had a wheelchair seat?
One bottle of this marvelous cure,
Changed my life that fast,
The things I said I now repent,
But they are in the past.
I didn't believe this guy last night,
I thought his a crooked deal,
But now I know he speaks the truth,
In his selling spiel.
Take my word. Listen closely,
He tells it straight and true,
I'm buying a dozen bottles myself,
Of this amazing brew."

——— o ———

The rush to buy was frenzied now,
Selling went on apace,
Buyers crowded around the stage,
Oblivious of what took place.
Something about this miracle's speed,
Disturbed my sense of right,
I felt a bothersome, gnawing doubt,
That I hadn't had last night.
For this reason I kept an eye upon,
The rejuvenated gent.
I saw him sidle to the left,
And slip out of the tent.
I followed, keeping out of sight,
To see what he would do,
A smaller tent was pitched behind
To house the working crew.
In he went and disappeared,
Voices could then be heard,
I moved to be in earshot then,
And picked up every word.

——— o ———

"Sounds as if your act went well,
You set 'em up real good,
You'd better not lay it on too thick,
Or it won't work as it should."

——— o ———

"It's an easy way to make a buck,"
The deceiving actor replies,
"It's almost too easy to pull the wool,
Over these hayseeds eyes."

——— o ———

I'd heard enough. My,feelings then,
Were simply overpowering,
I walked away in deep disgust,
My belief in people souring.
My disillusionment was complete,
I was utterly confused,

At seeing people's faith and trust
So flagrantly abused.
I thought of what my friend had said,
He saw them as they were,
While I'd defended them against,
What I considered slurs.
To me they'd looked as honest as
Other men I knew.
Now I feared that some of them
Might be crooked too.
Perhaps you find my innocence,
Childishly immature,
Sophisticated as you are,
Wise to crooks before.
Now my eyes are opened up,
Man's darker side disclosed,
Sad to learn that virtue is really,
Rarer than I'd supposed.
This devastation has shaken me,
This sickness of heart,
How like the loss of a treasured friend,
When innocence departs.
I'm sorely in need of comforting words,
My bewilderment is great,
Won't someone help me to understand?
You see, I'm only eight.

FRIENDSHIP

How precious friendship,
What jewel a friend;
More love to give
Than one can spend.

And so you stand
In worth to me,
And so I hope
You'll always be.

INNOCENCE

No time in life can ever compare
With those days of innocence children share,
When the world is as wide as the neighborhood,
And right from wrong vaguely understood,
When trust is the jewel awarded all,
And play is the days's most urgent call,
When the least liked word in the language is "NO!"
And tears stand poised for instant flow,
When a dirty face looks up in trust,
And a scolding wounds like a rapier's thrust,
When fairyland has reality,
And the loss of a pet spells catastrophe,
When clothes are soiled while the day's yet new,
And a conundrum is how to tie a shoe,
When a playmate's snub is the cruelest blow,
And the parental injunction is "eat and grow,"
When a mud puddle holds a tempting allure,
And the catalogue's toys are its cynosure.
When grimy fingers are mouthward bound,
And a bonanza is struck with a penny found.
When security's an arm around mother's knees,
And the daily admonishment is "say please,"
When the day's events go all amiss,
And consolation is a mother's kiss.
When eyes grow wide in astonishment,
And the loss of skin is a tearful event.
When the ABC's seem a seminar,
And hands get caught in the cookie jar,
When a somersault is a singular feat
And a goodnight kiss ensures sweet sleep,
But innocence, that attribute of the child,
Cannot with worldliness be reconciled,
As the morning's mist yields to the sun,
Childhood concedes to what's to come.

THE DOUR OUTLOOK

The population's growing fast,
Youngsters everywhere.
The school's so overcrowded,
Taxpayers feel despair.

The elderly hang onto life
Beyond four score and ten.
Nursing homes are bulging with
Women more than men.

Demographers are fearful we'll
Outstrip the food supply.
Defying odds we note that sex
Is at an all time high.

Heaven's roof is punctured now,
Somewhere above the pole.
Radiation's getting through
A man-created hole.

The environment's polluted so
That smog obscures the gaze,
Landfills spring up skyward with
Our plentiful castaways.

Social Security's in a bind,
People retiring early.
Even the weather's of concern,
Sort of hurly burly.

AIDS is sending many souls
To an early grave,
Others using harmful drugs
Become its willing slaves.

It's just a bit discouraging
When this list you scan.
Spacemen, can't you find for us
A brand new home for man?

LULU'S TALE (1988)

Prologue

Our tale enjoins the shapely ears
Of maidens set apart
By beauty, with its magic power
Of stealing manly hearts.
There was a day when beauties took
A calculated chance,
Aware that if they stole a heart
The law looked on askance;
Until a precedent-setting trial
Established for all time,
That stealing hearts of mooning swains
Was clearly not a crime.
Freed from culpability
By virtue of this decree,
Girls now uninhibited
Practice their thievery.
But, who struck down
That odious law?
Who is owed respect?;
To whom should girls in gratitude
And homage genuflect?
It's a tale of dogged courage
By a girl who stood accused,
Subjected to humiliation, and
Unmercifully abused.
How her pain brought sympathizers
Rallying to her cause,
How she clung with resolution
To hopes that hung by straws.
In the annals of your sisterhood
Her name belongs gold-starred.
Know her story, and hold her ever
High in your Regard.

LULU'S TALE

Herein set down is Lulu's Tale,
Inscribed in rhyming verse.
The epitome of beauty she,
Her loveliness her curse.
Chance made her the subject of
An historic fight,
Establishing forevermore
One inalienable right.
A winsome lass, so ravishing
That men stood goggle-eyed
Whenever Lulu hove in view,
And her perfection spied.
Her eyes were limpid pools of blue,
Her skin was white and fair,
Her lips were kiss-inviting,
And golden was her hair.
She lightly walked and sweetly talked,
Each gesture a queenly flair.
And yet, extremely reticent,
Reluctant herself to share.
Pursued she was most ardently,
Annoyed beyond all reason,
Pestered on excursions out,
Besieged in every season.
Proposals were so commonplace,
Some on bended knee,
That Helen of Troy was never wooed
With greater persistency.
Strange to relate, but as it was,
Not one her heartstrings petition,
To play there on that melody,
Loves recognized rendition.
Persistently repelling all
Who sought her "yes" to wed,
Some losers with a bad intent
Ugly rumors spread.
Others with darker purpose in mind,
Wounded deeper in pride,

Wanting revenge to salve their hurt,
A legal tactic tried.
Conspiring, they devised a plan
Congruent with their spite,
Humiliation to assuage,
Resentment to requite.
Headstrong and unprincipled,
Reprehensibly,
They leveled a charge against her
"Flagrant larceny".
Lulu they had arrested then,
In court she did appear.
"What is the charge against this girl?",
The judge demanded to hear.
"She broke the law," the conspirators replied.
"She stole our hearts away,
In flagrant disregard of law,
Justice demands she pay".
"You've heard the charge," the judge intoned,
On that you must be tried.
I ask you first, "are you guilty lass?"
"I am, Sir," she replied.
The trial was quickly ended then,
Admittance to the crime.
Sentenced, she was in a cell,
Doing prison time.
This rank injustice stirred unrest
Womankind appealed
For what she stole they avowed she had
Every right to steal.
A prestigious lawyer was employed,
The best known of her sex,
With reputation and success,
Commanding full respect.
On first appeal they might have won
Had not the judge his eyes.
He ogled Lulu indecently
Without the least disguise.
He ordered her to chambers next,
What happened we can't report,

But the judge returned a fuming mad
To uphold the lower court.
A despondent Lulu weary of
Her protracted stay in jail
Was freed by her defenders, who
Got her out on bail.
Lulu had withstood it all,
The tension and the stress,
So long on pins and needles though
Had cost her none-the-less.
One last resort yet to pursue,
The High Court of the land.
After deliberation they
Took her case in hand.
On 7th of May her case was heard,
Lulu standing mute.
On advice she wore a veil,
And donned a tawdry suit.
Outside the court the sister hood,
Defenders of women's rights
Clamorously were picketing
To the media's delight.
Inside the high-priced lawyer sat,
Pondering strategy;
Certain at last she had her chance
For immortality.
The Lower Court's decision she
Riddled like a sieve.
Stealing hearts, she asserted, was clearly
Lulu's prerogative,
Woman was made alluring, she said,
With intent to instigate
Propagation of the species,
So man would seek his mate.
Therefore, it was most obvious
The hearts that Lulu stole
Were legitimately pilfered
Fulfilling woman's role.
If then it was her inherent right,
The evoking of emotion,

Then hearts were never never stolen,
But surrendered in devotion.
The judges listened impassively
To the arguments pro and con.
No merit found in the plaintiff's case
Their verdict was foregone.
Womankind was jubilant,
Their precious right preserved,
Unanimous in agreement that
Justice had been served.
Imagine the strain on Lulu
Those months of fear and dread
She might have collapsed when the verdict came,
She proudly stood instead
She lifted her veil with trembling hands
As tears ran down her cheeks.
Expressive of the enormous relief
The first she'd known in weeks
Thrust into the limelight then and there,
Awash in adulation
Photographed and interviewed:
"Queen of Liberation"
Wealth and fame stood at her door
Knocking for admission
Lulu, in delirium,
Lacking sophistication
Was whisked away to brighter lights
Groomed to shortly be
An attraction to the public
For an admission fee
For many months thereafter
She toured the U.S.A.
Earning a place in legend
Extant yet today
Came the time her bubble burst,
Little cause for worry,
Her bank account was bulging.
All seemed hunkydory.
Men of stature sought her hand
Security helped decide

She yielded to a millionaire
The third among his brides.
Then one day she bore a girl
To dandle on her knee
A replica of her mother's charm
As pretty as could be.
"Everything I could wish for
Now belongs to me
Wealth and fame and happiness
A daughter, Melody"
Came a festering of relationship
"Twixt Lulu and her man
Who had his eye on No. 4
Flaunting the wedding band
Jettisoned was Lulu,
But with a parachute,
She got her child in custody
And a handsome sum to boot
A chalet in the country side
To which she now repairs
To soothe her troubled feeling
Alleviate her cares.
"Here can Melody lead a life
Free of intervention
Grow and flourish happily
Spared my tribulations
She's every bit as beautiful
As was I in my prime
Her engaging personality
Even more sublime
Oh, That she may never know
Other than happiness.
I'd give my fortune to that end
Could it avert distress
Fame and fortune have their price
In loss of privacy"
Arriving now was Lulu's time
To pay that penalty
Brief was her hoped for seclusion,
Fame has no hiding place

Men appeared out of nowhere
Suing for her embrace.
"These men who swear their love for me,
What is their incentive?
Can love of me rightly explain
Why they are so attentive?
Sadly, I can but conclude
As wealth is, so is beauty
Lures to fortune-hunting knaves
Who look on me as booty.
The one I chose not to refuse,
To whom I was a bride,
Like other possessions wearied of,
Cast me rudely aside.
Wealth I've known could be a curse,
Disrupting normal life.
I fear I never can be again
To any man a wife.
If beauty serves me badly,
Wealth adds to my burden,
Doubly jinxed I find myself,
Bereft of peace, that's certain.
The impositions thus imposed
Upon my guiltless head,
Spring not from my undoing,
Of circumstance are bred.
Best I concede to common sense,
Avoid what's not to be,
Devote my time and energy
To raising Melody."
Many are theories and practices
For raising the only child.
Which are effective, and which are not
Just can't be reconciled.
Lulu indulged her Melody's
Every whim and fancy
A method long regarded as
Being decidedly chancy.
A whipper-snapper she became,
Every shenanigan tried,

Tears to flow as wanted,
Tantrums when denied.
The blemish of her impudence,
The tarnish of vanity,
The taint of unbridled wilfulness,
Her offending repartee.
She earns a reputation with
Those who take her measure,
As daringly adventurous,
A seeker after pleasure.
The news came in the dark of night,
A sheriff at the door.
Lulu responding to his knock
Fell fainting to the floor,
The car had left the roadway,
Had struck a roadside tree,
Two were badly injured,
One was Melody.
Death long hovered o'er her bed,
Eventually restored,
Pathetically disfigured
Of her wildness cured.
A livid scar defaced her cheek.
Aided by a cane
She hobbled on two mangled legs
In excruciating pain.
She stood before her mirror and
Tears welled in her eyes.
The price of her foolhardiness
Belatedly recognized.
She languished in self-pitying
At loss of pulchritude,
Lamenting, allowed her peevishness
To sour her attitude.
Corrective surgery, comfort and care
Lulu lovingly provides,
But was there ever a doctor who
Could mend demolished pride?
The will to live stands balanced against
One's mental disposition.

The weight of bitter discontent
Disrupts its poised condition.
Wallowing in abject despair,
Cursing life as cruel,
Her body was found one morning
In the backyard swimming pool.
Lulu was hysterical,
Physicians shook their heads,
Torment raged within her mind,
A stroke, and she was dead.
Lulu the incomparable beauty,
Recipient of acclaim,
Time may increase her stature,
Cement her claim to fame.
Beauty fades as years go by,
Fame, 'tis said, is fleeting,
Money can't buy happiness,
Each here worth repeating.
So let us now inter our dead,
And close this tragic tale.
Be wary of life's pitfalls, girls,
And spare yourselves travail.

DE-BRIEFING

They played the songs of Christmas
My Christmas spirit rose;
But when I read the price tags
My Christmas spirit froze.
Now I'm known as Scrooge to some,
Who jeer at me because
I'm telling kids the truth this time:
"There ain't no Santa Claus."

The P.T.A. (1958)

Children, dear children
Our problem today
Is getting your father to P.T.A.
If he is grouchy
Remind him of lunch
Coffee and doughnuts
I'd say on a hunch.
Something to eat always pleases a man
And tell him about it as nice as you can
If he is happy, as seldom we see,
Maybe you'd better just leave it to me:
So I can mention the ladies there'll be
Flitting and flirting
And serving the tea.
This may induce him
To dress in his best
And smile and look happy
Along with the rest.
Really, he can be quite charming, I'd say
The younger the ladies, the sooner that way.
Don't mention the program,
The speaker, ignore,
He dislikes the business
He calls it a bore.
Now children, dear children
Please heed what I say
We must get your father to P.T.A.
'Cause once he is there
He will have a good time.
He will talk, he will chatter,
Be charming and fine,
I won't see much of him
And when we must go
I'll find him unready
And painfully slow.
Then children, dear children
A month from today
We'll handle the problem

In much the same way.
Be ready and helpful
Mark well what you say
And we'll get you father to P.T.A.

CONSOLATION

A life's but a blip on a TV screen
Where Endless Time's recording,
A split-second showing
A coming and going
Doomsday's statistics assorting.
But, as the centuries roll on by,
An occasional flash may show
A DaVinci, a Locke,
A Shakespeare, a Bach
Will leave there an afterglow.
As a sound is said no sound at all
With out an ear to hear it;
So the rose but wastes its lovely scent
Unless a nose is near it.
So genius becomes a mocking gift
Without the faceless horde
To audience, applaud, acclaim
Its uniqueness to reward.
But justice with its even hand
Can be compensatory.
We are the electors who proclaim
Who sits that throne of glory.
Let us then uplift our heads
Look genius in the eye
Let admiration flow unchecked
But envy, let it die.

CONTRITION

In youth, implicitly he believed
The righteous life could be achieved.
Setting sail to reach that goal,
He floundered on Temptation's shoal.
Wrongdoing, with magnetic force,
Had thrown his compass off the course.
Like many another whose good intent
Fell to temptation, he laments:
"Oh, I pray you, tell me why
It's in Man's nature to defy
What reason begs and right implores
To fall the victim to sin's allures?"
As if bidden, from out the sky,
The Voice of Wisdom makes reply:
"Because you're human, so inclined,
Since Eve, the first of womankind,
When tempted by a wily snake
Condemned us all by her mistake;
Stripped us of our innocence;
Lost Eden's blissful inheritance;
Doomed us to strive ineffectually
To heed the rules we'd best obey;
Charted us a zigzag path
That in its remorseful aftermath
Gives tongue to conscience to prick and chide
Like a martinet deep-housed inside.
This earth you'll inhabit all life long
Is a battleground 'twixt right and wrong.
That's the burden, as human beings
We've had to bear for countless eons.
Then let the good that you will do
Counterbalance what wrongs accrue.
Face up to life with a cheerful mien,
Dilute wrongdoing's inky stain.
Pay the penalty and don't complain
Beware! The ant lion's immuring pit
Snares fewer victims than Satan's wit.
Heed my advice, and do refrain

From ever paging me again."
With that, the Voice was heard no more.
Advice, the bane of the immature,
He pays little heed to Wisdom's advice,
And concentrates on his own ordeal.
Resorts instead to a human ploy,
Like many another obstinate boy.
He gropes to contrive an alibi:
"Others do things I wouldn't try;
I didn't act with bad intent
To do the wrong I now repent."
Then, as if suddenly perceiving its use
From Wisdom he extracts a new excuse
"What sorrier example could one conceive
Than was set for me by Mother Eve?"
Sensing his excuses sounded lame,
Failing completely to ease his shame.
Relief having only one open door,
Complete confession the only cure
He faced his mother and confessed
Made known to her what she had guessed:
"Mother," he said with a teary eye,
"Never again will I tell you a lie."

TELL ME WHY

Over and over I've asked myself
Why life's been so good to me,
With never an answer I'd consider
Satisfactory.
Ever the "why" intrigues me,
Preordained to be?
In life I've found no answers,
So deep its mystery.
Was I born to play a role
In the scheme of things?
A dispensation to fulfil
For He who pulls the strings?
Conceit, that known beguiler,
Might convince me so,
But the voice of reason counters
With its resounding "No!"
If then I'm but a sample of
What mankind can provide;
Why have blessings come to me
That others are denied?
Born to live in freedom's realm
Impelled to go as far
As ability could carry me,
To oblivion, to a star.
Health and vigor accompanying me
From the Horse and Buggy Age,
To now, when ventures into space
Have taken center stage.
Beholding my sons achieve their goals
On merit, ability,
Lived to enjoy their children,
Their children's progeny.
Known the warmth of a woman's love;
My employer's approbation;
Praise that came from a hundred tongues,
The rapture of standing ovation.
Acknowledged my deep indebtedness
To others I have known

Whose support was my assurance that
I never walked alone.
So great has my good fortune been
I'm in a quandary.
All because I don't know why
Life's been so good to me.

TO UNCLE SAM

What a kind old fella
Uncle Sam has come to be;
It's like we were related
He's so very kind to me.
I know I've never met him,
So it comes as a surprise.
How do you suppose he knows me
From a million other guys?
Yet once a month he sends me
A check to pay my bills

And keep me daily swallowing
The necessary pills.
I can't think why he does it,
Not that I would complain.
He must be very wealthy
If he can stand the drain.
Thank you, kind old buddy,
You in the striped-pantssuit.
You've kept me in the black, you see,
And eating well to boot.

VALENTINE'S DAY
1980

PERSON...   Ah, Cupid, how you stabbed my heart
            With arrow aimed so true.
            I just cannot accept the fact
            Your usefulness is through
            You tied me to a lovely lass
            And made the knot secure
            "For better of for worse", you said
            Which made our love endure
            How many knots, the like, you've tied
            While reigning absolute
            I fancy more than man could count
            Or angels could compute
            Say you, you're retiring now?
            No more to bend your bow,
            Or speed your arrows to their mark,
            I can't believe it's so.
            You've stood a monument to love
            While ages came and went
            You must be wrong in saying that
            Your usefulness is spent.

CUPID...   What you say is all too true,
            And not once over-stated;
            For romance owes me everything;
            But--now I am out-dated.
            These diff'rent times do frustrate me
            They kill my old desire
            So long the master of my trade
            A failure-I retire.

PERSON...   But Cupid, who can take your place?
            You with aim unerring
            Not Robin Hood nor William Tell
            Could match your skill and daring.

CUPID...   You speak so true; you are so right
            I'm matchless for a fact

If I retire, as of now,
My records stand intact.

PERSON...   Alas, I shudder at the thought
What ruin you will bring.
Lovers will but pine away
Without your arrow's sting
No! Assigned you are, eternally,
Never to retire
It's written thus, somewhere I know
In marble etched by fire.

CUPID...   Ah, me! Forever is a tiring word
Just think of all I've done
Another thousand years of this
Would weary anyone.
For ages flown--effectively
Heart I've tied to heart
In bonds of love, securely knit
For depth alone to part.
These days I'm saddened by despair.
My task,no longer fun
It's like I'm tying slip knots, now
So quick they are undone.
When smitten by my bow and barb
Commitment makes them shrink
Their wedding vows remind me of
A ship that's launched to sink
I've wondered in my musings if
Divorce gets any quicker
Why shouldn't I quit tying knots?
And use the modern zipper.

PERSON...   Surely Cupid, you must jest
Your work we highly cherish
Desert us now, and you must know
We humans all would perish
We've named a day to honor you
We call it "Valentine"
You recognize your alias

The heart is its design.

CUPID...   Honors! Honors! I've had many
            My problem isn't there
            Divorces, live-ins, woman's rights
            They bring me to despair

PERSON...   You've served too long, my cuddlesome
            To yield to grim despair.
            You know the pendulum swings back
            Disasters to repair.

CUPID...   Suddenly you're making sense
            That argument is sound
            You've quite convinced me I must stay
            And hope that day comes 'round.

PERSON...   Oh, good! How dreary life would be
            Without you to inspire,
            It's love that makes the world go 'round
            And sets our hearts on fire.

CUPID...   Now I'll level with you friend
            You've had nice things to say
            Once my duty was assigned
            It was mine to stay.
            As gods, we can't be choosers too
            I led you on, I fear
            That flattery you spread so thick
            Was wonderful to hear.

PERSON...   Shame on you for teasing me.
            You had me worried sick
            Just knowing Cupid's back at work
            Has made me well that quick.

CUPID...   Dear me, friend! I've talked too long
            My work is piling high
            Be of cheer. I'll do my best
            To make young lover's sigh

My bow-string's taut, my aim is fine,
My quiver's full of arrows
I fly so gracefully that I'm
The envy of the sparrows
The warranty has not run out
On all my moving parts
Another thousand years it's good
Against all fits and starts
Still, my thoughts do trouble me
I might turn renegade
These lawyers and their quick divorce
Are ruining my trade.
I'd like to beat them in the ground
Or pull out all their hair
Considering what they've done to me
T'would be no more than fair.

PERSON... Come Cupid! No such thing you'll do
You know as well as I
You'll ply your trade the same old way
Those lover's knots to tie.

CUPID... I suppose--well, here goes then
Another thousand years
Farewell friend, I'm on my way
Consoled, it so appears. (Leaves)

PERSON... Oh lovers, how you owe me now
For keeping Cupid busy
Soothing him is difficult
When he is in a tizzy
See, there he goes, back on the job
Of tying hearts together
Make your love endure or you'll
Undo my kind endeavor
And Cupid may defect, I warn
No sweethearts, then would marry
We'd cast all valentines away
And cancel February.

Read below!
Still confused? See #26, pp. 166-7.

Scandal ?

It is reason enough for one to suspect a person who puts feathers on arrows, whispered to have danced with joined hands secretly, to be guilty of shameful or wicked behavior. It should then surprise no one to learn that she thereby acquired a bad case of excessive saliva. If one is aware of her repeated attempts to obscure this evidence behind a smoke screen of confusing or obscure excuses, resulting in her shameless and annoying lack of discrimination, he should be further convinced.

Add to these revelations her deficient fish eating appetite, that she indulged in reading horoscopes at intervals, is said, on good authority, to speak at length in corners, and in addition is rumored to keep a carpet in her bedroom; then he who still doubts that she is nothing other than a slightly unbalanced, saucy and impudent person must be declared alert to meaningless flattery and not affected or influenced by quackery.